Dad's and Mum's Little Soldiers

Geoff "Tank" Todd

Published by the Todd Group

CAUTION

The content of this book is for parents, legal guardians or adult family members to provide safety and security training for their children.

Family Army instructors must fully read and understand the included teachings and be confident, ready and prepared to instruct their children before commencing training. This requires them to practice the skills to achieve competency in their delivery before training their children. They must be not only confident and competent to instruct the included teachings but also in the safe delivery of the included skills.

It is the family member instructor's responsibility to ensure their children are mature and responsible enough to be instructed in the included tactics and skills.

The contents of this book are meant for prevention of adult threats to children or as a last no-other-option resort, instructions are given for the use of physical counter actions to neutralise such threats.

It is the adult family instructor's responsibility to ensure the training is delivered and practised safely and that children do not abuse or misuse the included principles, tactics and skills.

The skills could injure or incapacitate and must never be misused or abused and should only be used within the laws of self-defence.

The author and publisher expressly disclaim any liability for any death, injury or damages the user of the book may incur. The author and publisher also expressly disclaim liability from death, injury or damages to third parties from the use or misuse of this book.

All rights reserved. No content of this manual may be copied, reproduced, stored in a retrieval system, in any way, in any form by any means, without prior consent in writing from the author and publisher.

This manual may not be circulated or distributed in any form or presentation, binding or cover other than its original published state.

© Todd Group 2024

ISBN 978-0-473-68977-3

Publisher: Todd Group

Author: Geoff 'Tank' Todd

Army Elite Forces Close Combat Master Chief Instructor

Depot: Self Defence School, a Department of The Todd Group

Phone/Fax: +64-3-477-8902

Email: coms@toddgroup.com Website: www.Toddgroup.com

DEDICATION

I dedicate this book to the military expert instructors who provided me with the training and qualification to have not only a career instructing the military elite in armed and unarmed combat and military self-defence but also the knowledge and capabilities to write doctrine, develop tactics and skills, write training and management programs, design training equipment and weapons, write training manuals and develop other forms of aide memoires and training resources.

The extensive training and qualification lineage from the military leaders in their field included below provided me with the depth of knowledge to develop doctrine and the tactics and skills that make up doctrine and training programs and packages.

This background ensured that I knew how to problem solve as part of threat neutralisation for wide ranging roles and under equally varied threat categories and situations, including underdogs facing overdog high-risk threats.

Being trained and qualified by the military close combat tradecraft best had always been my objective. In my thinking there is no substitute for anything less than the best of battle-proven training.

These Military Self-Defence (MSD) and Close Quarters Combat/Battle (CQC/CQB) lifelong proponents of our trade-craft include the following:

      The late SGM Harry Baldock

      The late Platoon Sergeant Charles Nelson

      The late Col Rex Applegate

I wrote this manual for parents to be able to train their own children with the same ethos and duty of care I received under the instruction of my former instructors.

I consider my role as the Master-Chief Instructor of the schools of instruction under the Todd Group HQ command a serious responsibility and a commitment to do my very best to arm all understudies with the most proven, safe and effective capabilities to protect themselves.

I give loyalty and respect to my early instructors and mentors and all my later military CQC/CQB/MSD Master-Instructors.

TABLE OF CONTENTS

- FOREWORD viii
- PREFACE ix
- ACKNOWLEDGEMENTS xiii

INTRODUCTION 1

- SLOW IS FAST IN LEARNING AND PERFECTING SKILLS 5
- ORDERS/INSTRUCTIONS/INFORMATION 9
- FAMILY ARMIES 13
- KNOW YOUR ENEMY 13

ANTI-THREAT TACTICS AND SKILLS 15

- YOUR FAMILY HOME IS YOUR FAMILY FORTRESS 17
- ANSWERING THE PHONE 18
- SOMEONE IS AT THE DOOR 20
- HOW TO REPORT AND REMEMBER WHAT YOU SEE 21
- IDENTITY PROTECTION 23
- ONLINE SAFETY AND SECURITY 24
- FAMILY ORDER NUMBER ONE 27
- STANDING ORDERS AND INSTRUCTIONS FOR SCHOOL 29
- LOOKING OUT FOR YOURSELF AND YOUR FRIENDS 34
- REPORTING INCIDENTS TO THE POLICE 34
- IDENTIFYING AND RESPONDING TO DANGER AWAY FROM YOUR FAMILY FORTRESS 35
- BAD TOUCHING 36
- SAY WHATEVER YOU HAVE TO SAY TO STAY SAFE 37
- PUBLIC TRANSPORT 38

- A LOOKOUT MAKES YOU SAFER: PUBLIC TOILETS AND CHANGING ROOMS 39
- VEHICLE ENTRANCES, ELEVATORS AND DOORWAYS 41
- FAMILY ARMY PLANNING, PREPARATION AND PRACTICE 43
- ESCAPING AND EVADING DANGER SAFELY 45

COUNTER-THREAT TACTICS AND SKILLS 46

- WARNING FAMILY INATRUCTOR! 47
- STRONG MINDED AND READY FROM YOUR BRAIN TO YOUR BOOTS 48
- THINGS YOU NEED TO KNOW ABOUT STOPPING A BAD BIG PERSON HURTING YOU 53
- FIT AND READY 54
- SAFETY IN TRAINING 54
- NEVER ABUSE OR MISUSE YOUR SKILLS 55
- THE POWER OF POSITIVE THINKING AND BEST OPTION DECISION MAKING 55
- LITTLE SOLDIERS' STANCES 56
- EVASION AND ESCAPE 58
- LITTLE SOLDIERS HIT THE DECK 64
- FOOTING RECOVERY 68
- STAMP KICKS 69
- PRACTICING LEG STAMP KICKS SAFELY 72
- STAMP KICK TO THE SIDE 78
- STAMP KICK FROM A SIDE ON FRONT STANCE 79
- STAMP KICKING TO YOUR REAR FLANKS 80
- LEAD LEG STAMP KICK TO THE FRONT 82
- TOE-OF-BOOT SPIKE KICKING 83
- STAMP KICKING FROM A KNEELING POSITION 84

- STATIONARY GROUND STAMP KICK 86
- GROUND OBLIQUE STAMP KICK 88
- GROUND LEG STAMP AND OBLIQUE STAMP KICK 89
- CQC SIDE FALLING AND GROUND STAMP KICKING 90
- GROUND MOVEMENT 91
- PREVENTING BEING GRABBED AND HELD 92
- RESISTANCE/COUNTER BEING HELD, PUSHED, PULLED AND LIFTED 95
- COUNTER ABDUCTION RESISTANCE 101
- COUNTER ABDUCTION RESISTANCE & SIDE FALLING FROM FRONT ON 103
- COUNTER ABDUCTION RESISTANCE & SIDE FALLING FROM SIDE ON 105
- COUNTER ABDUCTION RESISTANCE & SIDE FALLING FROM BEHIND 106
- VEHICLE/HOUSE/BUILDING ABDUCTION PREVENTION 110
- COUNTERING A REAR FLANK BODY HOLD 115
- COUNTERING A BODY HOLD FROM THE FRONT 121
- COUNTERING A BODY HOLD FROM THE SIDE WITH BOOTS & MITTS 125
- COUNTERING BEING ABDUCTED BY YOUR ANKLES 128
- HOW TO PROTECT YOURSELF AGAINST STRIKES 130
- NOT ALL DOGS ARE SAFE 132
- FAMILY ARMY INSTRUCTOR METHODS OF BREAKING THE BITE 137
- LAYERS OF PROTECTION 147
- FINAL ADVICE FOR YOUR LITTLE SOLDIERS 161
- INSTRUCTOR TRAINING PROGRAM FOR YOUR LITTLE SOLDIERS 161
- EPILOGUE 168

FOREWORD

"Geoff Todd and myself first met during the late eighties when the army unit, of which I was then a member, recognised the need for a wider capability from a close combat training programme than the old 'Kick and beat them until they're down then, kick and beat them until they can't get up!' variety, which was far more familiar to me during my younger days.

A much wider range of options for the many more roles that our modern soldiers can find themselves in, was now required.

Geoff's diverse background, including expertise in a variety of combat arts, as well as broad experience in the practical, no nonsense methods of managing people, whether they be hostile, hysterical or in danger; coupled with his lifelong interest and many years of research into the nitty gritty of the actual life or death struggles of soldiers at extreme close range where no rules apply; an interest that has taken him around the world to speak and train with those who gained hard won experience during conflicts from World War Two on; made him the ideal provider for this wider capability.

At his training facility, Geoff has a loyal team of practically minded, no-nonsense people who are equally eager to learn all they can of close combat while applying the acid test of, 'are these techniques easily learned and retained as well as being effective.' The team is not easily pleased.

For this, the book now in your hands, this same acid test was applied by Geoff and his team, using all of their experience from training, to develop their ideas for those most in need, the vulnerable, the underdog.

It was Geoff's aim that both adults, children and others who may be seen as 'easy prey' can, with minimum fuss, easily understand the instructions straight from the book and very importantly, know how, when and if to apply them. I believe that he has achieved his aim."

Former Sergeant Ron Evans

Ron Evans completed over twenty years' military service, including ten years as a paratrooper and a further ten in special forces. His active duty included tours in Cyprus, Southern Arabia, Zambia, Northern Ireland, Malaya and Dhofar. He was a member of a team tasked with the close protection of a royal family.
He was involved with the training of the New Zealand Police in aspects of close protection and was a military unarmed combat instructor.

PREFACE

Dad's and Mum's Little Soldiers is a two-part practical manual. It comprises anti-threat primary protection tactics to prevent children becoming the victim of bad big people's crimes committed against them, and when there is no out option and they are facing a bad big person, the employment of child-specific best counter threat skills of threat neutralisation. Threat neutralisation equates to not only physical skills to incapacitate a bad big person aggressor but as a first option evasion and escape to safety and assistance or physical counter skills to force a release or incapacitate a bad big person enabling evasion and escape.

Canine threats are extremely high risk to children. Having trained my own guard dogs and attack dogs over the years has enabled me to include a section on tactics and skills to deal with aggressive dog threats.

Counter actions must always be a last resort option when prevention or avoidance is not possible. The provided counter options to neutralise criminal threats have been specifically developed or adapted from our military self-defence methods and have been trialed and tested to failure to ensure they are the best and safest means possible for children under bad big person criminal threats.

Escape options prior to any physical contact are always the primary counter actions, however, if seized and under the threat of abduction, counter actions to affect a release and enable escape will be a last line of threat neutralisation.

This manual has been developed by me, Geoff "Tank" Todd, a lifetime proponent and instructor of military self-defence and military CQC close quarters combat. I have attained the close combat and self-defence rank of military Elite Master-Instructor and I am the Master-Chief Instructor of the Todd Group, the oldest private specialist training provider of our European-derived military elite armed and unarmed combat and military self-defence.

The Todd Group, formerly the Baldock Institute, began instructing our military self-defence and close combat in 1927 and has only had Harry Baldock, our founder, and I as the Master-Chief Instructors of the HQ facility over the past 97 years.

Harry was a NZ Army WWII military unarmed combat Chief Instructor and I have had over 25 years' experience as a military Chief Instructor to the military elite and regular forces.

Military self-defence and military CQC are not sports or arts and as such are based on dirty tricks brigade means and methods of threat neutralisation often by aggressor incapacitation. They provide even the underdog with the best chances of neutralising formidable foes.

I have been a military elite close combat Master-Chief Instructor as well as an instructor to specialist police and diplomatic protection and civilians. Over forty years' commitment to my tradecraft has provided me with thousands of hours of instructing time. It also comes with the responsibility of developing specialist tactics and skills in military self-defence and armed and unarmed combat.

I have trained tens of thousands of adult alpha exponents and proponents. Dirty or deadly military close combat skills combined with physical fitness and uncompromising mental toughness have given them the highest chances of defeating formidable foes.

Instructing such combatants and arming them with high-level threat neutralisation capabilities is considerably less difficult than training underdogs like young children, disabled persons or senior citizens.

I thrive on using my military self-defence and close quarters combat expertise and qualifications in training law abiding underdogs to overcome overdog assaulters, as this is challenging and extremely satisfying.

To develop and modify existing primary skills for children with the disparities in physical size and strength compared to criminal adults has taken over five years.

Skills have been tested to failure as there is no unarmed skill that can effectively guarantee every time it is employed that a child can neutralise an adult assaulter threat against them.

Many variables needed to be taken into consideration. The final selection of developed skills for this manual and the included content under testing proved to be the safest and best means.

Skills competency and confidence are not the only vital factors in overcoming adversity. Mental toughness and protecting oneself at all costs is what empowers the provided tactics and skills.

Parents as instructors must train their children to know what they have to do and how to do it until they can make the decisions and execute them without fear, hesitation or self-doubt.

The underdogs will have the element of surprise on their side and must take every advantage of this as they will not be expected to attack their attacker with dirty tricks that can incapacitate them.

The Todd Group is a specialist private training provider with an over 95-year commitment to our tradecraft. We do not, however, have the capabilities to provide mass instruction globally. This is why this manual has been published for parents or guardians to be family instructors to their children.

I am the Todd Group Master-Chief Instructor and I consider my role and position a commitment and responsibility and not just a job or hobby. I have a duty of care to provide understudies with the best chance of winning, not merely surviving.

I am available for contact with any questions family army instructors may have.

coms@toddgroup.com

Military CQC Master-Chief Instructor Todd Group

Geoff "Tank" Todd

ACKNOWLEDGEMENTS

I would like to show appreciation to the people that assisted me with writing this manual.

My wife Trish for all artwork as well as supporting this and my many other undertakings and projects for over forty years. Trish also proofread and provided editing from a mother's perspective.

Professor Timothy Crack for all his advice and assistance with editing and proof reading.

Head wrestling coach at the Combat Sports School Caleb Steven for providing his own children and his young wrestlers for the testing and proving of *Dad's and Mum's Little Soldiers* in-house developed skills.

Todd Group second in command Master-Instructor Kowley "Cowboy" Mitchell and family for also assisting with skills testing and proving.

Todd Group exponents, proponents and instructors that assisted with proof reading and skills selection testing.

Senior Instructor Phase 3 Specialist proponent and instructor Sean Lancaster who has tirelessly assisted with IT and technical aspects as well as proof reading. Sean has been a constant supporter and assistant of *Dad's and Mum's Little Soldiers* along with my other work.

Phase 3 Specialist proponent and Instructor Paige Gale for proof reading.

Advanced exponent and Instructor Karina Devereux for proof reading.

All ranks at Todd Group HQ that assisted with trialing, testing and proving or eliminating skills.

INTRODUCTION

This manual is for family army instructors and your little soldiers. To distinguish between the instructor content and the little soldiers' content we have used two different fonts.

- Instructor content font.

- Little soldiers' content font.

Family army instructors need to read all instructor content and your little soldiers' content prior to reading through and explaining your little soldiers' content to them.

Dad's and Mum's Little Soldiers is a family army safety, security and self-defence program to protect your little soldiers against bad big people.

It is designed to stop bad big people from hurting your little soldiers.

The tactics and skills in this manual are drawn from our military self-defence and military unarmed combat training packages. They have been modified and adapted to give your little soldiers the best and safest means and methods of avoiding, preventing or, as a last no-other-option resort, countering threats against them.

Some skills have been specifically developed for children because of the disparity of their physical attributes and capabilities compared to bad big people.

Physical size, limb lengths and strength disadvantages have meant that adult skills had to be modified or specific skills developed for children facing threats from bad big people.

<u>Anti-threat</u> tactics and skills are designed to prevent you ending up in a threatening situation in the first place, and they are the best way to stay safe because they avoid physical contact. <u>Counter-threat</u> skills are emergency skills for when you cannot prevent or avoid danger; They always carry more risk.

The selected skills had to be primarily very specific to anti-threat preventative methods and means or evasion and escape under threat to maximise safety.

This is necessary because of the high risk to children targeted by bad big people. Educating your little soldiers on the dangers bad big people present to them and arming them with knowledge on such threat recognition is very important. Making sure your little soldiers understand the importance of following family army anti-threat orders and instructions to keep them safe is very important.

Military unarmed combat training for adults in self-protection includes combined offensive and counter offensive strategies. For children, however, anti-encounter preventative tactics are the priority and if compromised and under threat, evasion and escape tactics and skills are primary threat-neutralisation practices.

Footwork in this children's self-protection training package has been selected for its straight-line advantages or because the movement is something that children can easily adapt to and quickly achieve proficiency at, like pivoting to face an escape direction.

Running footwork is faster and covers more ground than stepping fighting footwork. So, it should be employed immediately under threat to evade and escape the bad big person, as it is the best and safest option to stop the threat.

Children do not usually have the physical capabilities to employ combative skills with a high level of threat neutralisation, especially against a fully-grown adult with criminal intentions. The skills in this manual have been selected and specially developed because they increase safety and are generally little soldiers' primary best means and methods to fit with their physical attributes and capabilities. They provide the primary means and methods of preventing or countering threats that your little soldiers may face from bad big persons.

This package is specific to threat avoidance and threat prevention by escaping and evading criminal adult threats against children of a predatory sexual kind, including abduction. As a last resort, simple proven counter-attack gross motor skills are given to hinder or stop the attack.

Such counter skills make your little soldiers harder targets, increasing the chances of good big people coming to their assistance and of the bad big person being caught.

All physical counter-action skills in this manual are included in case the little soldier has already been compromised by being confronted, contained or seized and secured. If seized and secured, they need to evade and escape their adult attacker and part of the strategy to cause their attacker to release them is being capable of employing the counter skills in this manual.

It was important that only the best, safest and most proven means of stopping a bad person attacking your little soldiers are included in this training program. Less is more in military self-defence. So, having one skill that is a primary proven means to combat or counter wide-ranging threat types and threat situations is better than having many different options.

You need to understand that in unarmed self-protection nothing is one hundred percent guaranteed to neutralise threats. The skills in this book have been selected and developed because they are user and situational specific to children and the threat of abduction. The physical counter skills purpose is to cause incapacitation and as such disengagement to enable evasion and escape.

Your little soldiers' legs are their longest and most powerful limbs, and their boots are their best and most robust bodily weapon. Stamp kicking (to be defined later) is the best destruction-producing and pain-producing means against an adult attacker, for the following reasons.

- Stamp kicks are a gross motor skill requiring minimal physical coordination capability but producing the maximum destructive output.

- They can be employed from standing, kneeling or lying down on the ground.

- They can be employed to keep an aggressor at bay, make them release their hold on your little soldier, to incapacitate a bad big person by destroying the integrity of the knee joint or kneecap ligaments, to cause decentralisation or at minimum to cause excruciating pain.

- They can be employed at close or point-blank body contact range and at an attacker to their front, side or rear flanks.

- When targeting the lower leg, stamp kicking can keep the bad big person at bay or cause knee joint or kneecap ligament injuries that are incapacitating.
- They provide maximum counter-reach, keeping the bad big person out of grab-and-hold range, or can cause a release of a grab or hold.
- When effectively employed, stamp kicks cause extreme pain at a minimum and can cause incapacitation, aiding in escape.

Alternatively, the genitals can be targeted with knee strikes or heel of boot rear flank donkey heel kicks when seized and secured from the rear flanks. These cause autonomic reactions, pain and can affect a release of a hold on your little soldier.

When seized and secured in belly-to-belly holds, the eyes can be targeted as part of an escape strategy.

There have been many considerations taken into account in the development of this manual specific to your little soldiers' age, size, strength, physical capabilities and the dangers bad big people with bad intentions present.

By practising a single primary threat neutralisation skill against wide ranging threat situations, your little soldiers' skill competency and confidence will be as high as possible and as such, their chances of effectively protecting themselves will be at their very highest level. Having single skills to prevent or counter entire threat categories means less confusion in skill decision making and as such less likelihood of error in skills selection. Knowing how to best target the eyes, groin and lower legs will make decision making as simple and easy as possible.

It is very much a matter of identifying the closest available target and setting up and executing the skills that provide the best chance of incapacitation and evasion and escape.

Obviously not all children are of the same physical build and physical capabilities. While some may be small and fast and hard to get a hold of, others may be heavier and not as physically fit and fast, and as such may need to use hard target tactics including falling and ground stamp kicking to prevent being abducted.

SLOW IS FAST IN LEARNING AND PERFECTING TACTICS AND SKILLS

Your little soldiers should practice tactics and skills in parts initially. Then they can combine the parts as they achieve confidence and competency, eventually completing the entire skill execution in one fluid action. As they gain proficiency in the skill execution, reduce the number of parts until the entire skill is practiced in full on the command "Go!" As they gain in confidence and competency, increase the speed of the skill execution.

Martial arts and combat sports are competed in gender categories, age groups and weight divisions and there are rules, officials and safety practices. Military unarmed combat and military self-defence, however, are not governed by any of the previous restrictions. As such, they give the underdog the best combative chance of neutralising a formidable foe.

Military CQC (Close Quarters Combat) and Military Self-Defence (MSD) are military tradecrafts and not an exact science. They provide the best battle-proven chance of threat neutralisation for a soldier facing a formidable enemy, even when wounded or taken prisoner. They provide the best combative chance of threat neutralisation under unpredictable threats, even for an underdog.

Little soldiers, your safety and self-protection are very important to your family army and to me.

I want to give you only the best and most proven training possible. Therefore I have developed this manual based on the best of my army unarmed combat and self-defence tactics and skills, specifically developed or adapted for little soldiers.

"Less is more" in tactics and skills and only the best, most proven means for little soldiers to make and keep themselves safe are acceptable.

"Slow is fast" when it comes to learning and practicing tactics and skills.

Learn skills slowly in parts then in full when you are confident. Increase speed only when you can practice the skill safely and without error.

Always remember your dad and mum want the very best in life for their little soldiers and they want to keep you safe. They know they cannot be with you all the time to protect you, and this makes them worry. So, they have gotten you this little soldiers' family army training program developed by me, Tank Todd, to help keep you safe. I have been an army self-defence and army unarmed combat Master-Chief Instructor who has trained big soldiers for over 25 years. Your dad and mum want the people who train big soldiers in the real army to help them learn how to best train their little soldiers.

Not everyone can go to the Todd Group and be trained in army self-defence and army unarmed combat by me and my training team.

So, this little soldiers' basic training program is something little soldiers can be trained at home to learn from, with the help of their family army instructors (who could be their dad, mum or older brothers and sisters, or other caregivers).

Soldiers in the army know that training is a task to be continued and not a project to be completed. Like them, you must never stop training to make yourself as safe as you can be.

Families that live together need to plan, prepare, and practice together to make themselves safer. They need to be safe inside their family fortress (that's their home), and safe away from their family fortress. They need to be able to protect themselves against bad big people. So, you must take part in your training with enthusiasm, attention to detail and with commitment. That's an order, and good little soldiers always obey orders from trusted big people.

Your family army must have plans, tactics, skills, orders, and instructions to make everyone safe. Every family army is different. So, you must work with the big people in your family army to write plans and orders that work best for your family army.

Just like big soldiers in the army when they must use self-defence and unarmed combat to defend themselves, the risk is high and their best chance of stopping the danger if they cannot avoid it is made possible by their prior training in army self-defence and army unarmed combat.

I want you to be serious about your safety and self-protection training. That is why I have written this manual like a very young person's version of an army unarmed combat training manual.

Your family army instructors can read and explain to you the training orders and instructions in this little soldiers' safety and security manual. They will also be your instructors for all your training and you must listen carefully to them and like big soldiers in the army you must take orders and listen to instructions. You must do what you are told correctly and at the very best and safest training level you can.

I want you to train the army unarmed combat way. So, I have included a lot of words and terms specific to army unarmed combat and army self-defence in your *Dad's and Mum's Little Soldiers* training manual. Your family army instructors will help to explain these words to you.

Although real threats where self-defence is needed are not common, knowing how to prevent ever being a victim of such threats is your best insurance to stay safe.

I hope that you will never have to put a stop to a bad big person trying to hurt you, but it is very important that you know how to stop a bad big person hurting you if it does happen. You will have the best chance of staying safe if you take this training seriously and practice the army self-defence and army unarmed combat way.

Just like the army where self-defence and unarmed combat is a last resort option, it must be prepared and trained for and you need to do the same. So, get on with it little soldiers!

ORDERS/INSTRUCTIONS/INFORMATION

Family army instructors read and explain the following to your little soldiers.

Little soldiers must be able to talk to trusted big people in their lives if they feel something is wrong or they do not feel safe.

Little soldiers must tell trusted big people if anything happens that hurts them, makes them worry, makes them feel bad about themselves or makes them feel sad. Little soldiers must also tell trusted big people if anything like this happens to their friends or family members.

Trusted big people must listen to everything little soldiers tell them. They must tell little soldiers that telling them what has happened was the correct thing to do.

Trusted big people must not interrupt little soldiers when they are telling them about bad things that have happened to them or that made them feel bad. Instead, trusted big people must listen carefully and never put words into little soldiers' mouths or impose their own suggestions on their little soldiers. Trusted big people must make little soldiers feel safe and secure so that they are comfortable telling them everything.

Trusted big people must then let their little soldiers know that they are proud of them for telling them what has happened.

Trusted big people must tell their little soldiers not to worry and that the big people in their family army will make sure that they're safe.

The little soldiers' trusted big people in their family army must write down accurately the details told to them by their little soldiers.

Family army instructors will most likely have to inform the police or important trusted people in your little soldiers' life of what your little soldiers have told you and this must be on a need-to-know basis and must be correct and accurate.

Bad big people might be strangers, or they might be people that you know.

Bad big people who do bad things to children know that what they are doing is wrong and they may try to get you to keep it a secret. You must tell trusted big people in your lives of this wrongdoing even if nothing serious happened. No matter what bad big people tell you to do or not to do, you must tell your big trusted people what has happened including telling about being asked to keep secrets. There must be no secrets with strangers as there is no good reason for you to have secrets with strangers. There also must be no bad secrets with anyone you know.

If ever you get a gut feeling (that is, something that makes you feel uneasy inside or makes you think something is wrong), even if nothing bad happens, make sure you tell trusted big people everything.

You must always stop strangers getting close to you and you must not let kind or soft words make you drop your guard and trust a stranger, as they could be a bad big person.

Some bad big people know how to talk nicely and kindly and will do so to make you feel safe and gain your trust.

Never let strangers get close enough to touch you and always keep your eyes on them. In the training chapters of this manual, you will be instructed in tactics and skills on how to keep yourself safe.

Never let strangers get inside your head and gain your trust by believing what they tell you is true. Never accept anything from a stranger, like food or sweets or gifts.

If you feel uneasy about a stranger, then go with your gut feeling and remain silent and avoid them.

Do not tell strangers anything about you. There is no reason why a stranger should know your name, who you are with, what you are doing, where you are going or any of your personal or family details.

Regard such questions as suspicious and stay alert and silent. Keep out of their arms' reach and avoid them.

Put as much distance as possible between you and them immediately.

Remember to report such suspicious behaviour as soon as possible to a trusted big person in your life. If you can, write down all the details immediately after the incident.

Never forget your family army orders and instructions, and make sure you use them to keep yourself safe.

Remember, if you do not tell a trusted big person in your life how you felt and tell them the details about the stranger that made you feel uneasy, then you are not doing the correct thing. That stranger may approach you again with bad intentions or do harm to some other little soldier.

Remember you have done nothing wrong. Never feel upset or embarrassed about doing the correct thing and telling a trusted big person in your life everything.

Your family army must know everything that happens to you so that they can protect you. Even if you think small details do not matter, these details may be very important for the police to catch and stop the bad big person that tried to get close to you and gain your trust.

Little soldiers must be brave and must never keep bad secrets from trusted big people.

Little soldiers have a duty to report bad things so that they can stop the hurt and stop bad big people from harming little soldiers. Reporting bad things can stop more bad things, or worse bad things, from happening to you or to other families' little soldiers.

Dad's and Mum's Little Soldiers personal security and anti and counter abduction training is a very serious subject, providing possibly a last line of protection against the very serious threat of abduction to your little soldiers.

Parents need to determine when their little soldiers are old enough to understand the rules and responsibilities when it comes to the skills practice and usage in this manual.

Your little soldiers need to understand that the skills taught here are not to be used against other children. These skills should only be used in training with their family instructors or against a bad big person to protect themselves against harm or prevent abduction.

By looking at your home security and any risks to your little soldiers when they are not with you and are away from home, you should be able to determine when your little soldiers are at increased risk and need to be trained in the *Dad's and Mum's Little Soldiers* tactics and skills.

If your little soldiers, when starting school, could be in situations where you or a responsible adult are not there to protect them at all times, you should seriously consider instructing your little soldiers before they start school. Initial training may just be in specific anti-encounter tactics that reduce risks, in line with the times and situations where they could be exposed to danger.

Bad big people abduct not only young children but also teenagers. So, the *Dad's and Mum's Little Soldiers* training is applicable to five-year-olds through to teenagers and young adults.

Look at your little soldiers' personal security, appearance and demeanour through the eyes of a bad big person. Honestly evaluate what would make them vulnerable to being molested or abducted, and eliminate or reduce such risk factors to the lowest level humanly possible.

If your little soldiers are very immature and cannot take this provided training seriously, especially if they cannot be trusted to train safely or may well abuse and misuse the skills, then you should instruct them in the anti-threat preventative components of this manual only, until they are mature and responsible enough to be instructed in the counter measures.

Family army instructors need to read this entire manual carefully and practice the skills for yourself before instructing your little soldiers.

Make sure your training area is safe and you have a soft surface to train on along with a tackle bag, punch bag or a soft padded impact target like a big cushion for practising stamp kicks on. Use of such equipment is depicted later in this manual.

When you go through the manual instructing your little soldiers, focus on one tactic or skill at a time and make sure your little soldiers fully understand security and anti-threat tactics first and foremost, before last-resort physical counter skills are covered.

Make sure you have them practising safely and slowly at first, in part and then in full, and only increase speed once confidence and competency are demonstrated.

Make sure skills are practised with attention to detail, accuracy, correct range and with maximum safety.

It is very important that your family army instructors have read through this *Dad's and Mum's Little Soldiers* training manual and have practised and prepared the training sessions.

FAMILY ARMIES

Family armies are all different. Some have mother and father instructors, some have just fathers or just mothers, and some have stepfathers or stepmothers.

Some family army instructors will be older brothers or sisters or stepbrothers or stepsisters or grandparents.

Little soldiers and family army instructors alike must take family army training seriously.

Little soldiers, you must listen carefully to your family army instructor or instructors and do what they say, always giving 100% in attention to detail, training, safety and effort.

KNOW YOUR ENEMY

Bad big people can do bad things to little people for lots of reasons.

Bad big people don't always look bad, and they might talk nicely to you or ask you things that are believable like have you seen their missing little boy or girl, puppy or kitten.

Bad big people might offer you things that they know most children would like, such as chocolate or toys.

Bad big people might even try to say that they are friends of your family.

Therefore, your family army orders must always be applied when it comes to strangers or things you think may not be true.

Always look and think carefully. If you have a feeling that something seems wrong, or could be wrong, use your family army tactics to keep yourself safe.

Always assess, always think, never guess and never forget to use your family army tactics to keep yourself safe.

If something makes you feel uneasy inside, go with your gut feeling.

Avoiding or preventing danger by using your family army orders, instructions and tactics is the safest and best way to keep yourself safe.

Threat prevention (that is, stopping a bad thing from ever happening) is safer than having to use counter-threat skills (that is, having to use unarmed combat self-defence skills to get you out of a bad situation).

Any time you have to use counter skills to stop being harmed, abused or abducted, the risk is high and you could get injured or abducted.

Always remember your family army orders and instructions and use them to keep yourself safe. Do not let kind looks, soft words or treats make you break from your orders, instructions and tactics that are there to keep you safe.

Some bad big people have problems in their brain. They may have been born with brain damage or they may have developed it because of an accident. Some of them have become bad because bad things have happened to them in their past or they have been brought up by bad big people and had a bad home life.

Some bad big people do bad things to little people because they take bad drugs or drink alcohol.

There are many reasons why bad big people want to do bad things to little people and the best way for you to ensure this does not happen to you is to not concern yourself with trying to guess if or why big people are bad or not. Instead, just use your family army orders, instructions and tactics to prevent them being able to do anything bad to you.

ANTI-THREAT TACTICS AND SKILLS

Prevention is better and safer than having to use counter actions.

There is an old army self-defence saying that "prevention is better than counter." Anti-encounter tactics through planning, preparation and practice ensure you do not end up in a bad situation. Your family army orders and instructions will include areas and places you must not go, or you must go around or move through quickly, staying alert and keeping out of harm's way. These risky locations will have been identified by your family army advance legwork, which means walking the routes you will take and identifying areas that are high risk. Some high risk or danger areas will be identified by doing research. High risk or possible danger areas will be written into your safety and security orders as no-go areas. Avoid or rapidly pass through these areas carefully.

Anti-encounter preventative tactics ensure bad things can't happen to you and as such are much better than having to defend yourself once a bad thing is happening. So, you should always be thinking "I can prevent bad things from happening by avoiding identified danger areas or by being alert, identifying possible danger as early as possible and getting away from it." This way of thinking is the best and safest thing you can do to protect yourself from bad big people.

Use your brains to outsmart bad big people by being aware and alert.

If you see anything that makes you feel uneasy, including when you get a gut feeling that there could be danger, then you need to get out of harm's way immediately.

Live by your little soldier safety and security tactics and skills at home and away from home, making sure there are no opportunities for bad big people to get close to you.

Do not take risks as it is better to be safe than sorry.

If you ask yourself how a bad big person would think, you can identify danger areas, suspicious people and vehicles in advance and avoid them. Wherever possible employ anti-threat preventative tactics and skills to identify danger and avoid it. Never take chances with your safety and never approach any person, dog, vehicle or danger area when you can avoid such dangers. Doing so can avoid the consequences of a bad decision.

Knowledge is power and you must use your new knowledge to make and keep you safe.

YOUR FAMILY HOME IS YOUR FAMILY FORTRESS

Your home is your family fortress, and it must keep bad big people out.

There must be family army orders for answering the phone and for answering the door.

Your family must decide on plans and orders and then make sure that all little soldiers stick to the plans and follow the orders and instructions. If you fail to obey orders, there will be a punishment.

Just like the case of big soldiers in the army who disobey orders, your punishment might be pushups, sit ups, running, or extra household chores like peeling potatoes, washing dishes, sweeping, or vacuuming.

ANSWERING THE PHONE

Phone calls are supposed to be answered by the big people in your family army.

If you must answer the phone and the caller turns out not to be a friend or family member that you know and trust, then you must know the standing orders to follow.

Make sure, before you answer the phone, that you have a pen or pencil and writing paper at the ready to write any details down.

Do not answer the phone by saying your name. Instead, when answering the phone, you can say "Hello, who am I speaking to?" and then after they speak you can say "If you just wait, I will get one of my parents."

Be polite, but don't tell strangers more than this. Never tell the caller about yourself, your family, where you live, who is currently at home, or who lives there. So, never give out any personal information to strangers on the phone.

If you are home alone, tell the caller "My parents are busy right now. Can I take your name, phone number and a message and get them to call you back?" Another option is that if you are home alone, tell the caller that "I'll just go get my daddy or mummy," then walk to the other end of the house and then turn around and walk back to the phone and say "Daddy (or mummy) is busy right now and cannot come to the phone. He (or she) has asked me to get your name, phone number and a message and he (or she) will get back to you."

If the stranger does not give you his or her details but asks any other question say "Sorry, I must go and help my daddy or mummy" and hang up.

This is not a lie; It is a tactic to keep you and your family army safe.

Have your home alone phone answering orders and instructions clearly written down or printed out beside all phones in your family fortress and your notebook or writing paper and pen or pencil there as well.

SOMEONE IS AT THE DOOR

You must also know what to do if the doorbell rings or if there is a knock at the door of your family fortress.

First, do not open the door of your family fortress. Quietly go and tell a parent, older brother, or older sister in your family army that someone is at the door. So, you must alert one of the big people in your family and let them check on who is at the door and decide if it is safe to open the door.

Do not open the door to anyone if you do not know who is at the door.

Do not open the door if you think it is a stranger at the door or someone you do not trust.

Little soldiers must also keep their family fortress safe and secure by not leaving doors, windows or gates open that should be closed and locked.

HOW TO REPORT AND REMEMBER WHAT YOU SEE

Good little soldiers must report anything they see that doesn't seem right, like strangers outside looking at or looking around your family fortress.

Be alert and aware of unknown cars parked outside or close to your family fortress. Keep an eye out for suspicious cars driving up and down and passing your family fortress slowly.

If you see strangers or bad big people hiding, sneaking around, or trying not to be seen near your family fortress, then you should look at them out of the corner of your eye. Do not look at them directly, because this lets them know that you have seen them.

Act as if nothing is wrong and as if you do not even know they are there. Then quietly go and tell one of the trusted big people in your family army that there is something wrong.

Try to remember things about the car and the stranger you saw.

You can remember how big the stranger was by comparing him or her with someone you know, or by comparing them with someone in your family army.

It can be confusing, but not all bad big people will look big or bad. Some bad big people will try to trick you by looking nice and by acting friendly. They may even appear old and harmless.

Bad big people can be male or female. They can be young, not so young, or older. They might even be a man and a woman working together to try to abduct and do bad things to you.

The standing order is that if you do not know them, then you must not trust them, and you must follow your family army orders and instructions.

If you know them but do not trust them or do not feel safe around them, the same family army orders and instructions still apply.

Your family army wants to stop bad big people from hurting you, and from hurting other little soldiers. You can help to stop bad big people if you can describe them, or describe their clothes, or describe their car. This information can help your family army and the police to catch the bad big people and stop them hurting anyone.

If you can remember the colour of their hair and what clothes they were wearing this would be helpful information. But remember safety first! Remember that moving away from danger is a standing order and you must always follow your family army standing orders.

Make up a funny story in your mind's eye about the person as this will make it easier to remember things about them. Here are some examples.

The wizard had a grey baseball cap or a bald patch, was skinny and as tall as Uncle Jack, with a long pointy nose, funny striped pants, and a shirt the same colour as our garage door.

He had a big tear in the right or left knee of his blue jeans like a wild dog had bitten him. Things like this tell the police he not only had blue jeans, but the knee was torn and this could make it easier to identify him.

IDENTITY PROTECTION

It is important to protect the identity of your little soldiers by not putting their name on clothing or school bags where it can be easily seen.

Such information could help bad big people to get close and to mislead your little soldiers by calling them by name.

ONLINE SAFETY AND SECURITY

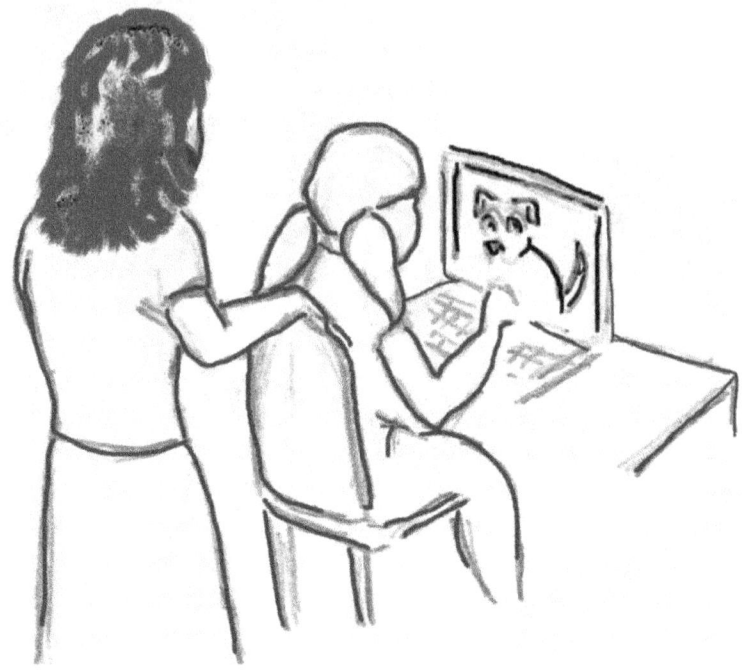

Family army instructors, take advice from professionals to ensure you have the very best online safety and security software to block any access to objectionable material. We are not all highly skilled in IT and need to get professional assistance to provide online security and safety.

Family army instructors, it is a good idea to password protect any online-capable device. Log your little soldiers on and monitor their browsing regularly as well as checking their browsing history before logging them off. Family army instructors need to oversee online use of computers and devices and instruct your little soldiers to report anything to you that they feel could be bad.

Little soldiers, you must never give out computer passwords or any security or safety information online. Little soldiers, you must always go online in the presence of big people in your family army and never go online when big people in your family army are not aware and present.

Little soldiers, you must not take any device away from family areas in your family fortress where you are not in the presence of and under the supervision of big people in your family army, and you must only search for acceptable material. If something upsets you online or is bad, do not delete it. Report it and show it to the big people in your family army immediately. Little soldiers, treat all online activity just as if you were facing a stranger, where you would not tell them personal information or give away family information that could affect your security or your family's security or safety. Apply your *Dad's and Mum's Little Soldiers* family army orders and instructions for home and out-and-about safety and security to all online activity.

Remember, anything posted online can be there forever and can reappear at any time. So, don't put personal, sensitive, or embarrassing information online about yourself or anyone else. Protect the safety and security of your family members and friends by not putting any details or information about them online.

Do not post photos or video footage online, this includes on social media, unless it has been checked and approved by your parents.

Any people you communicate with online must be approved by the big people in your family army and must be included on your online trusted friends and family members email list. You must not communicate with anyone online that has not been approved by the big people in your family army. The identities of all cyber friends must be proven and confirmed by big people in your family army. The big people in your family army will want to make sure everyone you have contact with, either online or in person, is safe, including friends, family members, and friends of friends.

Just like when you get a bad gut feeling about someone you meet in person and must report everything about the person and what they have said or done, the same applies to online messages and chat. Remember, it is easy for people to hide and pretend to be someone they are not online. If you do not know them in real life, you should not have any contact with them online. They may be sending you chat and pretending to be your age and to share in your interests, but they could be a bad big person in disguise.

Never agree or arrange to meet anyone you do not know and trust that you have been communicating with online. Never ever agree to keep secrets or agree to secretly meet anyone you know only from online chat. Do not have cyber friends that are not friends that you know well in real life. Make sure that the big people in your family army have met and know them and their family and have approved of you communicating with them online.

Big people in your family army must know not only your friends, but friends of your friends, and their families. Never post personal information about yourself or your family on social media or provide information about your personal or home life or give away safety and security information. Just like reporting everything that makes you feel bad, sad or unsafe in real life, the same applies to anything online. Never be embarrassed or afraid to show big people in your family army anything online that you feel is suspicious, bad or wrong. Big people in your family army must be able to keep track of web sites and material that you are accessing online.

Little soldiers, you must immediately show big people in your family army if you receive any pictures that are rude or about sex, including text and messages of a rude or sexual nature. If you receive any messages that are threatening, including bullying, you must report and show them to big people in your family army immediately. There are laws against supplying sexually explicit material to children and there are laws against cyber bullying. Big people in your family army can report objectionable material and inappropriate communications to the police and can advise your internet provider. Your internet provider and the police can then take action to ensure that this wrongful behaviour stops immediately.

The best way to stay safe little soldiers is to abide by the orders and instructions of your family army when it comes to social media, surfing the internet, and using online communications. Treat all online usage the same way you would treat dealing with the unknown dangers of communication and contact with strangers.

Little soldiers, never try to change computer or online settings and do not clear browsing history or delete anything that makes you feel uneasy, embarrassed, upset, or unhappy. Show it to big people in your family army right away.

Do not open any unknown attachments you receive or click on any received links. Ask big people in your family army before you do anything that is unknown and not approved. This could stop computer viruses infecting your devices.

FAMILY ARMY ORDER NUMBER ONE

Safety first always and above all else.

Little soldier, you must understand that if you see something suspicious, then calmly, as if you do not know anyone is there and as if nothing is wrong, move away like you are playing and have not seen anyone and report what you have seen to a big person in your family army.

If you see a car that is parked suspiciously, or that is driving slowly up and down past your family fortress, then try to remember the colour of the car, and what type of vehicle it is. Is it a car with two doors or four, is it a truck, van, station wagon or a utility vehicle (that is, a ute)?

Collect information only if you can do so without being seen to be doing so. To do that you need to be sneaky. So, look out of the corner of one eye and get as much information as possible.

Write down what you can remember as soon as it is safe to do so. Write it in your family army notebook or notepad by the phone. If you can write down the registration plate number, or even just part of it, this will be very helpful.

You could use your finger or a stick to record the car registration number in your garden.

If you cannot write a license plate down, try to memorise it by putting the letters and numbers into a funny or silly picture in your mind's eye so that you simply cannot forget it. For example, MMDW12 might be Mickey Mouse Drinking Water at midnight, or FJL8 might be Fried Jelly Lizards have 8 fingers.

If you have a mobile phone, being a hi-tech little soldier, you could enter the registration number into your phone, but you must do it covertly. Yes, "covertly" is another army word that means without being seen, like a sneaky squirrel.

Your family army notebook and writing stick are a very important part of your little soldier kit. To remember details accurately you should write them down first and then immediately report it to a big person in your family army. You can use concealment to write down details from inside your family fortress when you feel uneasy about strangers or unknown cars outside your family fortress.

Remember always to act as if you are not aware of a strange car and any strangers by slowly, calmly and quietly going back to your family fortress and reporting what you have seen to one of the big people in your family army or to a trusted big person in your life. You could discreetly use your cell phone to call your family members inside your fortress and report the details.

Keep distance between you and any suspicious big person and pretend you are unaware of them and are just playing in your front yard.

Use concealment by moving behind a fence, bushes, your family car or a tree inside the yard of your family fortress to write down information. This is a good tactic to get information about strangers acting suspiciously or strange cars that don't belong in your street. They may be parked with someone inside looking out or they may be driving up and down your street slowly.

If you have one of those fancy smart phones you can covertly take a photo, do so only if it is safe to do so and you cannot be seen and can get away if you need to.

You must have decided at a family army meeting who are the trusted big people in your life. So, you need to write down their names in your family army instructions and orders book as well as in your notebook. Remember to write down their contact information. You'll need their phone numbers at home, work and their mobile number.

You must also memorise your list of trusted family army big people allies.

You must also decide on a secret family army code word. The secret family army code word will be used if your mum or dad or big people in your family army cannot pick you up from somewhere (like school, a friend's house, the movies), including in an emergency, and if they must get a person from your trusted big persons family army allies list to meet and transport you.

Your dad, mum or the big people in your family army will give the family code word to your family army trusted allies, and you will ask them what the code word is when they come to meet you: "What is the code word please?" If they do not know the code word, then you must not go with them until you can contact your family and get consent.

You must think of the code word as an emergency safety and security word or words for emergencies or unforeseen circumstances.

It must be something that you cannot forget.

You must memorise and never forget your secret family army code word.

After the secret family army code word has been used once, a new secret family code word will need to be decided. That's because after it has been used once, it is no longer a secret.

STANDING ORDERS AND INSTRUCTIONS FOR SCHOOL

Attention little soldiers, I repeat: you must remember the secret code word that your family army will tell a trusted big person from your list of trusted big people. Sometimes a trusted big person may have to collect you from school, or somewhere else, when your parents need to change plans and break routine. This can happen at short notice or in an emergency. If, however, that person's name is on the family army trusted big persons' list, and they know the secret code word, then you will be good to go. These standing orders are important to keep you safe.

Your family army instructors must give the code word to the chosen trusted big person from your list of allies, and they must be able to tell you the code word on request.

Your family army big people can make changes to the orders and instructions in this manual if they know it is safe to do so.

If you get dropped off at school, then go straight into the school grounds.

Never let strangers get too close to you near or at school or anywhere else. Never go with strangers or take anything from strangers.

Bad big people are sneaky. They know what children like. So, they will tell you things and they will try to give you things to trick you into thinking that they are nice people.

Never take drinks or sweets from strangers. Never go with strangers who tell you that they are looking for their lost dog or cat or something like that. Never let the latest electronic games or electronic gadgets make you drop your guard and forget about the dangers of bad big people.

Again, remember that bad big people may be men or women. They may also be a man and a woman working together.

They may be teenagers the age of your big brothers or sisters.

They may act in some way so that you do not feel threatened or unsafe.

They may have a friendly dog with them or even another young person.

Preventing something bad from happening is a much safer thing to do than having to get away or defend yourself from a bad big person when something bad does happen.

So, stay ready, quietly alert and aware. Keep your distance from strangers. Move back and to one side or move so as to put a barrier between you and the suspicious stranger. That barrier might be a car in the street, playground equipment in a playground, a park bench, a lamp post, or anything solid.

You may need to move around a barrier to ensure a bad big person cannot get close to you.

Never get close to a car or get into a car that you should not get into.

If something feels wrong in any situation, then quickly move away and get away. Then report what happened to a trusted big person as soon as possible.

After school, you should wait inside the school grounds inside the fence, until your transport is parked and ready for you to get into. If you see any strangers around your school who are acting suspiciously, go and tell a teacher or someone in the school office right away.

Your family army needs to have discussed and agreed upon the safest way to get you to and from school. This is part of your family army movements plan. For example, if you walk to and from school, then you should do so with your friends or your brothers and sisters. That is because there is safety in numbers; bad big people would rather try to hurt you when you are alone than when you are with other people. Make sure you know and follow every day the decided safest route that is part of your family army movements plan.

At your family army planning and preparation meetings, identify safe places you can go to if you feel uneasy, unsafe or if something bad happens on your way to or from school or anywhere else.

Safe places and people include police stations or your local shop, or someone on your family allies list who is known and trusted in your community. Keep in a group of friends moving together. Yes, move in a formation and let your friends know if you see or feel something is wrong and let them know of anything you see that could be a danger to you or your friends.

You may have to be a brave little leader and tell your friends what to do if something is wrong to keep you all safe. Never accept rides in cars from strangers or from people you know unless your family army big people have agreed that these are trusted big people, and unless they can tell you the secret code word.

Always make sure even in an emergency or when plans are changed with no prior notice that trusted big people from your family allies list can tell you the family army secret code word before you go with them.

Keep your distance, ask questions and get the correct answer before you get close to anyone in any car and never get into a car before you are certain it is the right thing to do and is safe to do so.

In any emergency where immediate help is required and you cannot contact big people in your family army or get help or assistance from one of your trusted persons from your family allies list, common sense must prevail.

A schoolyard accident where a teacher must take you to the emergency room or an accident in the street where a concerned citizen comes to your aid are two such examples.

Get your teacher, the citizen or emergency services personnel that have come to your aid to call your parents if you are not able to yourself and get them to speak to your parents.

An order is an order, and you must obey family army orders and follow plans at all times except in immediate emergencies or situations where your safety or security requires immediate intervention from caring good big people.

LOOKING OUT FOR YOURSELF AND YOUR FRIENDS

Always look out for your friends because they might not have their own family army, and they might not be trained in what to do or have family army orders, instructions or a plan to follow.

If you see them in danger, then warn them of the danger and try to get them to stay with you and your friends. Remember, there is safety in numbers.

If your friends are in immediate danger from a bad big person, then take a quick look and try to remember things about the bad big person (their appearance, skin colour or ethnicity, clothes, car, etc.). Then quickly go to get help for them by heading straight to the closest safe place and by telling a trusted big person everything.

REPORTING INCIDENTS TO THE POLICE

If you have a mobile phone and you, your friends or your family are in danger, then get yourself out of any immediate danger and call the police.

When you talk to the police on the telephone, remember to breathe and stay calm. Try to speak slowly and clearly, telling them who you are, where you are, and what is happening. Listen to what they say and do what they tell you to do.

Don't ever risk taking photos or video if there is any likelihood of being seen; Remembering details and getting away from danger is more important.

In New Zealand the emergency services phone number is 111. If you do not speak when you call this number your call will be directed to a recorded message of instructions to undertake. Once connected to police, the police call taker will attempt to communicate with you by asking simple yes or no questions and you will be asked to push any keys on your phone in response to these questions. If you are not able to speak, listen carefully to the questions and instructions from the call taker so they can assess your call and arrange help for you.

If you can, it is always best to speak to the call taker, even if you have to whisper. You may need to whisper to give your location.

If you are living in another country, or visiting another country on holiday, it is important that you know how to contact local emergency services there.

IDENTIFYING AND RESPONDING TO DANGER AWAY FROM YOUR FAMILY FORTRESS

Stay alert, keep your eyes open, looking around you everywhere for danger. If you identify danger, then make sure that you move away and keep away from the danger, going instead to a safe place.

As part of your family army plan, you must report in (go home, or call home or call your parents) if you want to make any changes in plans. You must get permission from your dad or mum or other caregiver before you change any plans.

Keep your eyes open when you are at the park or at a playground as well as when you are going to or coming back from any place away from your family fortress.

When you are away from your family fortress and in public places, you need to be more alert and more careful than you do in the security and safety of your home. You will not be so familiar with places away from home so don't take risks.

In the evening when it is getting darker, remember that the risk of bad things happening to you is higher because bad big people often try to use the cover of darkness to hide or sneak around. So, you should never be out alone after nightfall.

You must always follow your safe little soldiers' plans, instructions, and orders. This will make you much safer and can stop bad big people from getting near you.

Always think in advance and plan so as to make sure that bad things never happen to you.

BAD TOUCHING

Never let any big person you do not know or trust get close enough to touch you. To stop a bad big person touching or getting hold of you, move away from them, creating a safe distance and keep your distance from the bad big person.

If a bad big person, or any person, touches you in a bad way, get away and tell dad, mum or another trusted big person. Sometimes meeting and greeting or bidding farewell to friends, family or friends of your family will include a hug or handshake and this is perfectly normal and respectful.

Sometimes when you have achieved or just partaken in sport, hobbies or schoolwork you will get handshakes, hugs or a pat on the back.

However, strangers without proper reason should not be touching you.

Even when a big person touches you with good reason like meeting, greeting, bidding farewell or congratulating you, if that interaction includes bad contact or bad touching that you feel and know is wrong you must immediately get away and let trusted big people in your life know.

No one should touch your private parts, press or rub their private parts against you, show their private parts to you or try to make you touch their private parts. No one should show you pictures of peoples' private parts.

Some bad big people might try to mask their bad touching or bad behaviour as part of friendly interaction. If their behaviour involves contact with, or touching or showing private parts, however, then it is very wrong of them to do this, and your duty is to report it to trusted big people.

No bad big person has any right to grab hold of you and try to make you do something you know is wrong or try and forcefully take you with them.

Aggressive contact like grabbing, holding, pushing you down or pushing or pulling you away like into a car, a building or behind trees and bushes means you are in immediate danger. Lifting and carrying or dragging you away as well as any striking, slapping or kicking action means you are in immediate danger of being abducted and harmed.

Bad big people might be abducting you to molest you, which means to do things to you that are very wrong and very bad.

You need to do everything you can to get free, get away and get help. To do so you will need to have learnt, practised and perfected your counter abduction skills from this training manual until you have the best chance that you possibly can of being able to get free, get away and get help.

If you see someone nearby that can help you when you are in immediate danger, then escape the immediate danger and get that person's attention by yelling out "Help Me! Call The Police, Help Me!" Sometimes you may need to call out for help immediately before countering and escaping if a person that can help you can be made immediately aware. You need to raise the alarm before they get out of hearing range. If a bad big person is holding you against your will, and this may include bad touching that they are masking as friendly interaction and they won't let you go, then yell so everyone can hear "Help Me! Call The Police, Help Me!"

If you get the attention of any good big person, make sure they know exactly what is happening before it is too late because you will not be able to get their attention once they have moved out of hearing range or if you have been removed from their hearing range.

SAY WHATEVER YOU HAVE TO SAY TO STAY SAFE

Don't say anything to the bad big person about telling dad, mum, or the police on them. If they ask or tell you not to say anything to anyone, then you must be sneaky and tell them that you will not say anything if they stop doing it and let you go right away and never do it again. You must say whatever it takes to make them believe it, so that they stop hurting you and so that you can get away.

You can tell them you don't want anyone to know and that you will not tell anyone, and you can even ask them not to tell anyone.

After you get away from them, however, then you must get help by telling your dad, or mum, or a trusted big person as soon as possible. Do not be embarrassed to tell a trusted big person exactly what happened.

PUBLIC TRANSPORT

If you are taking the bus, then sit near the driver, where they can see you directly or where they can see you in the mirrors above their head inside the bus. If you can see the driver in their mirrors, then they can see you. You can sit beside a friend, or beside a family member or beside someone you consider safe. Never sit at the back of the bus or where the driver cannot see you.

A LOOK OUT MAKES YOU SAFER: PUBLIC TOILETS AND CHANGING ROOMS

Be extra careful around public toilets and changing rooms. That's because bad big people sometimes try to attack children in these places. You need to look, think, and decide before going inside. Anyone or anything that makes you feel uneasy or unsafe means that you need to get away.

This should be part of your family army plan, orders and instructions. "Evade and escape" is army talk for getting away and staying away from the danger. Then you need to report it. Tell a trusted big person who can help right away. Safety is with your family army or with trusted big people.

Staying away from risky places and away from danger areas comes before anything else. This is one of the most important parts of your family army safety and security plan and orders.

If you or a friend have to use a public toilet or changing rooms, you can be a lookout for your friends and they can be a lookout for you, watching out for you and you for your friends to make sure you are all safe. If anything happens, you can raise the alarm for each other and get help quickly as this is most important.

Because a dad cannot go into female toilets with his daughter and a mum cannot go into male toilets with her son, the following is a sound security and safety practice under such circumstances.

You go into the toilet, check it is clear and safe and then return to the door where your family member can see you (or just call out) to let your family member know that it is all clear and safe.

If you enter to check that the toilet is clear and safe and do not call out within five seconds, your family member outside will conclude that you are in danger and will come charging into your aid. (This five-second rule must have been agreed upon in advance.) Therefore, it is important that you should always follow all orders and instructions exactly.

Your tactics as part of your orders and instructions are not for misusing. So, never fool around with them as you could cause trusted people in your life to come to your aid and this could cause problems for them and get you in a lot of trouble.

When they know you have someone outside that can come to your aid or raise the alarm, bad big people are less likely to try and harm you.

If you are using the toilet and a bad big person tries to harm you get out of there, or if you can't, call out to your family member immediately "help me, get the police, help me!"

If you are with one of your young friends and need to use a public toilet your friend must stay outside close enough to hear you call out to them and be able to see the toilet entrance/exit.

You can check the toilet is clear and safe and call out to them that it is and they can confirm that they have heard you.

If anyone tries to do you harm, you can call out to your little lookout friend, "help me, call the police" and they can raise the alarm and get help immediately. This buddy system is good for security and safety and as a deterrent to any would-be bad big people with bad intentions.

Any time you do not call out that the toilet is clear and safe your little lookout should call out to you again. If you do not answer they should raise the alarm immediately.

Make sure your friend maintains their position outside the toilet until you exit, and if they want to use the toilet too, you can swap roles and be their lookout. The same applies to your dad that cannot enter female toilets and your mum that cannot enter male toilets. They can be a lookout and you can call out that the toilet is clear and safe to them, and they can confirm they have heard you.

VEHICLE ENTRANCES, ELEVATORS AND DOORWAYS

You do not want to be hit by a car when you are walking on the footpath/sidewalk. So, checking to make sure that vehicle exit ways (or driveways) are safe to cross is another important little soldiers' requirement to stay safe.

When approaching a vehicle exit way, move away from the exit way and closer to the curb side of the footpath so you can look diagonally into the vehicle exit and see if a vehicle is approaching.

When entering a building, walking through a doorway, or entering an elevator/lift, you need to check for danger. When entering buildings, doorways or elevator doors, stand back 2 m (6 feet) on your side of approach so you can look diagonally inside at the far side of the elevator, open doors or building entrance way. Then stay 2 m out and pass to the other side of the doorway or entranceway to look back diagonally from that side to the back of the doorway or entranceway and determine if it is safe to enter.

This diagonal corner-to-corner both-sides visual check of the entrance and immediate interior will keep you out of arms' reach and harm's way and ensure that you can avoid any dangers waiting for you just inside.

FAMILY ARMY PLANNING, PREPARATION AND PRACTICE

Get your family army to write down for you in your family army safety, security and protection notebook things to look out for. Get them to explain to you about bad things and bad people. That way, you will know what to look out for and who and what to stay away from.

Your family army, under the command of your dad or mum, must work with you in writing your little soldiers' plan that has orders and instructions on how to avoid bad big people and what to do when bad big people try to hurt you.

You need to practice, practice, and practice your anti-threat tactics as well as your counter skills as a family unit. Do this until you cannot get your tactics and skills wrong, and you cannot forget them or your orders and instructions. The same goes for knowing your secret family army code word.

It is planning, preparation, and practice that helps to stop bad things happening.

For example, your family army plan and family army safety and security orders must identify danger areas to be avoided. By doing some legwork with the big people in your family army, you will be able to walk to places you must go to or go past and identify dangers and risks. Your family army will be able to decide on ways to reduce risks in these areas and write them into your safety plan.

For example, the big people in your family army may have to find the safest route for you to take to walk to your friend's house, or to catch the bus or to walk to school.

Learn how your enemy thinks and acts by thinking how a bad big person could get close to you and hurt you. Thinking about and knowing how to identify bad big people and how they act is an important part of your advance planning and training.

Bad big people are sneaky. So, look for places they could hide. They want to get away after hurting children, so look for places they might use to get away. Think about places they could be waiting where they are hard to see until it is too late and stay away from such places.

They might be hiding, waiting for a child to come along so they can abduct them. They could be waiting in a car or van, so stay well away from suspicious vehicles and people. Avoid all unknown people and vehicles, as there should be no reason to go near them.

Make sure that when you are walking or riding your bike it's on a safe well-populated route.

Ask your family army members to point out danger areas to you.

Always remember that it is better to be safe than to be sorry.

Family army basic training involves practising your tactics and skills together repeatedly until you cannot forget them or get them wrong. This training will make you safer.

Planning, preparation and practice will make you a trained, ready and prepared little soldier.

Your training days and times must be planned in advance. Remind your dad and mum about your training if they forget.

Potential danger could be a concealed or a visible threat.

ESCAPING AND EVADING DANGER SAFELY

When you are escaping bad big people, make sure that your movements are towards and through well-populated areas. These should be well-lit areas with at least some people, houses, buildings and cars. This allows you to get away safely or get help if you need to.

Avoid going through dense forests or bushland areas and never do so alone or after dark. Rural areas on your own can be very dangerous if bad big people are waiting there for a lone child to come along.

If you are escaping a bad big person and you cannot get help or get to safety, you might have to hide. The first thing to do is to run and put distance between you and a bad big person that is chasing you. By putting distance between you and the bad big person, they will not know where you left the footpath or road.

If you cannot get completely away to safety, then find a hiding place where you can see anyone approaching but they cannot see you. When you hide, do it carefully so as not to leave footprints in mud or anything that would let the bad big person know where you are hiding.

If you are hiding, then conceal yourself well; yes concealment, this means to hide yourself so you cannot be seen. You need to be like a mouse in a forest.

Slow your heart rate by controlling your breathing, and stay alert. Breathe in through your nose and out through your mouth with low-level, controlled breathing cycles.

Bad big people do not want to get caught committing a crime so they cannot afford to stay at the scene of their crime for very long if that could lead to them being arrested. Hiding can make it difficult for them to find you; They may just give up and go away.

If you have a mobile phone, wait until it is safe and use it to call for help from where you are concealed. If it is not safe to talk, you can dial the emergency number for your country and remain silent but if the operator asks you to push a number on your keypad then you can do so.

Don't come out of hiding until you are sure it is safe to do so.

Come out from concealment slowly and carefully, moving as carefully as possible from one place of concealment to another.

Keep down low and move as silently as possible, stopping and looking to make sure it is clear of the bad big person.

Get to safety and raise the alarm as soon as you can.

COUNTER-THREAT TACTICS AND SKILLS

The primary objective is always prevention of harm by using your brains to outsmart bad big people. To effectively do this you need to plan to keep your little soldier safe and teach them how to avoid danger areas and recognise signs of danger.

Nothing is 100% guaranteed and with bad big person threats on children the risks and dangers are extremely high.

So, in the face of danger, smart, safest-possible-option decision making is essential.

As there is no single option that is the best means of countering all variations of same or similar threats several counter options are required to be effective against changes in threat.

These are listed in order of safety and effectiveness:

1. Evasion and escape to safety.

2. Stamp kicking and evasion and escape to safety.

3. Abduction prevention by ground falling, ground stamp kicking, ground footing recovery and evasion and escape.

4. If seized and secured and lifted off of the ground, counter actions to cause a release (eye spiking/kneeing groin) and safely sliding down to get boots on the ground and evade and escape or stamp kick and evade and escape.

These vital counter actions in order of safety and effectiveness will be reiterated throughout the threats counter actions content.

WARNING FAMILY INSTRUCTOR!

The skills selected and adapted for the *Dad's and Mum's Little Soldiers* self-protection and counter abduction program provide your little soldiers with the best chances of preventing or countering abduction threats from bad big people.

It is very important, however, that as parents and instructors to your little soldiers, you make sure that they understand their limitations and capabilities.

When facing a bad big person, some children simply may not have the physical capabilities to be able to effectively prevent or counter an abduction.

Children at such an age and size are vulnerable and need to be protected at all times.

Many skills that would be primary options for adults are not practical for children as they do not have the physical strength, length of limbs or the required mindset.

There is no guaranteed means of threat neutralisation, and the best option is always situation avoidance through planning, preparation and practice.

Against bad big person threats where prevention or escape is not possible, counter skills need to provide the safest means and methods to maximise your little soldiers' chances of getting away to safety.

This is not about fighting; this is about countering or combating a bad big person with the best and safest means of threat neutralisation. This may be by evasion and escape, or by countermeasures that break the bad big person's hold on your little soldier or by countermeasures that incapacitate them by targeting the eyes, genitals or ligaments of the kneecap or knee joint.

To effectively neutralise a bad big person, your little soldier requires mental toughness and must set up and execute the skills correctly. This is as good as it gets for the underdog against a physically superior overdog.

I have taken considerable time to ensure that the included tactics and skills are specific to little soldiers' capabilities and threat neutralisation requirements, so as to ensure they provide the best chances of threat neutralisation.

Just like training military combatants, the best tactics and dirty tricks provide the best chance of winning against a formidable foe and not merely surviving.

Dad's and Mum's Little Soldiers provides primary threat neutralisation capabilities by means of anti-encounter and physical counter and combat skills to prevent an assault or abduction by a criminal adult.

Combat skills mean attacking first to stop being attacked and counter skills mean under-threat counter attacking to stop the attack and escape.

Family army instructors, you must make sure that your little soldiers practice every skill slowly and carefully in parts and then in full until they can't get it wrong.

Only when they can execute the skill in full, slowly and correctly, will you instruct them to gradually increase their speed and commitment in practicing.

Always make sure the training area is safe and that your little soldiers train safely and sensibly.

In your safety brief, instruct them on the importance of being in range for counter actions executions and the importance of accuracy, so they do not miss the target and hyperextend their leg, which risks injury.

Little soldiers, we will now begin training you in how to stop a bad big person hurting you by countering the threat.

Countering the threat includes skills to evade and escape the bad big person as well as to stop them from hurting you.

If you have to use counter skills, then you are in a bad situation and you must be strong of mind and use the best and most proven skills to get away, get help or stop the bad big person from hurting you.

Attention little soldiers: you need to always make yourself as safe as possible in training, so you do not get training injuries.

Do what your family army instructor tells you and in the way they tell and show you how to do it. Always listen and pay attention to orders and instructions.

STRONG MINDED AND READY FROM YOUR BRAIN TO YOUR BOOTS

Family army instructors, your little soldiers need to be brave and to know how to control their fears and emotions if they are confronted by a bad big person.

All the skills in the world are worth little if your little soldier cannot overcome their fears of the threat. The most important component of escaping and evading or stopping violent threats is the ability to switch on maximum mental toughness. This ability requires an understanding of the effects of fear on the body.

The effects of fear on the body may include an increased heart rate, heavy breathing, tremors and changes in body temperature. These effects can make your little soldier stand stock-still and become incapable of escaping or of self-protection.

Make sure you tell your little soldiers about these effects and that their teeth may chatter, their thighs, arms and hands may tremble, or they may feel an upset in their stomach. They may feel helpless and they may feel like crying.

Let them know that as soon as they are in a situation of danger and feel the onset of the effects of fear, they must control their respiration by using slow controlled low-intensity cycled breathing: They must inhale via their nose and exhale via their mouth in a slow synchronised controlled manner to reduce or prevent the adverse effects of fear.

If they instead hold their breath or start hyperventilating, this can produce many negative effects, including tunnel vision, stress-induced audio exclusion (that is, the inability to hear anything around them), helplessness and a general inability to assess, think, decide and do what needs to be done to save themselves from harm.

Tell them to turn on all their senses: their eyesight, hearing and sense of touch and feel. A heightened sense of touch is especially important through the soles of their boots. It increases and maintains stability and mobility via the balls of their feet, making them ready to initiate an expedient evasion and escape or a committed deliberate counter action.

They must set a state of readiness. They must look and undertake an immediate threat assessment and situational assessment and decide on the best means of escaping and evading the threat. If this is not possible, they must decide on the best means of stopping the threat by making themselves a hard target or countering the threat with the skills included in this manual.

Tell them to be brave and to take control of the situation. They must make decisions that will make them hard to get hold of, hard to keep hold of and harder still to catch or abduct.

Make sure you tell them to be positive and to silently, in their mind's eye, tell themselves that they can and will get away and get help. This requires quiet self-confidence.

I use the acronym WAR (Willing Able Ready) for training combatants in my *Brain to Boot* mental toughness program for military self-defence and military close combat. Military combatants can repeat this to themselves silently in their mind.

You can choose a similarly short mind's eye silent means of self-reassurance. Perhaps it might be something like I WILL WIN or WINNERS NEVER QUIT.

Make sure they understand not to hold their breath, as this affects their physical capabilities as well as their thought process and decision-making ability negatively. Watch out for this bad habit when they are training.

Every action they take must be powered by mental toughness. Start with controlled respiration. Then your little soldier turns their senses on and assesses and decides on the best option to escape or to stop the bad big person.

When one sense is turned on, the other senses are turned up to a higher state of awareness and alertness. Because the threat will usually be identified visually by your little soldiers, the sense of sight is the top priority.

Mind's eye real time visualisation as part of deciding and reconfirming is very important for avoiding panicked decision-making.

When they are ready to execute their counter options, they should think READY, SET, GO!

The following evasion and escape and counter abduction set up initiation components will be instructed in the following counter skills components of this manual. They are very important and share commonality as they make your little soldier a harder target, more ready and a capable little soldier.

Counter skills must be initiated from a respire, squat-crouch, ready-set-go status.

If a directional change is required in an escape-and-evasion, then a respire, squat-crouch will be combined with a pivot action in the desired direction. Self-checks of a ready, set-to-go status include stance and footing. For specific-direction evasion and escape, a combined sliding footwork stance change and a pivot action will be required. Ensure that your little soldier makes footwork adjustments to be ready to initiate their evasion and escape or counter measures initiation.

Risk is reduced by maintaining a hard target ready status and by staying out of immediate threat range, or by using angles or barriers prior to initiation and execution of their decided option. Components for evasion and escape include a squat-crouch combined with synchronising their respiration with their sprint-start evasion and escape initiation. For counter options employments, continued cycled synchronised respiration throughout their decided counter skills options executions is essential if they are to perform at the required physical output levels and maintain physical capability.

The same ready, set-to-go practices apply to all counter action executions.

For example, to counter abduction if seized, use inhale, exhale, pivot, ground side fall, counter stamp kick, followed by footing recovery, evasion and escape, all conducted with cycled respiration and executed off of the squat-crouch ready-set-go status, and with directional pivoting if required. These skills will be explained soon.

Skills need to be set up, initiated and executed with attention to detail and commitment, to increase safety and your little soldiers' chances of getting away or stopping or hindering the attack. These primary components not only increase your little soldiers' chances of escaping or stopping a bad big person, but they also lessen time for slipping into the negatives of self-doubt, by having them undertake set ups and checks and re-checks.

Little soldiers, if someone comes up to you who makes you feel unsafe, you must discreetly identify the threat before they can get close enough to touch you. Start controlled breathing, think and decide which way to move to make yourself safer and to make yourself a harder target. So, think ahead, discreetly look ahead, and look around you and decide on the best way to avoid or evade and escape danger.

The Todd Group instructs big soldiers in how to be as mentally tough as possible from their brain down to the soles of their boots. This all starts by controlling your breathing when you are afraid. Breathing in through your nose and out through your mouth in a controlled manner can stop the effects of fear, like trembling and shaking arms, hands and legs, feeling sick in your tummy or your teeth chattering. It is important to stop the effects of fear so that you can make the best decisions to get away, or if you can't get away, to counter the threat. If you do not control the effects of fear, you might freeze and not be able to get away or counter the threat.

So as soon as you face danger, breathe in through your nose and out through your mouth in a slow and controlled manner to slow down your heart rate. You need to stop your heart from racing and you need to prevent heavy breathing.

Being as in control as possible will help to stop you from freezing through fear. You do not want to freeze and to not be able to move and to not be able to get away.

Being controlled and ready to respond will also help you to see and hear dangers and to help you to look, think, and decide on the best and safest options more quickly. Being ready and in control will also help you to remember a description of the bad big person, their clothes or their car, and their words and actions. Holding your breath, even for a few seconds, especially when using counter skills, can cause you to quickly lose the physical fitness you need to counter bad big people.

Think of it like ready-set-go before you run to escape. Breathe in through your nose as you squat-crouch down into a ready-set position and breathe out through your mouth as you pivot in the escape direction and push off sprinting off and away, or when you use a counter skill.

Using this military self-defence method of breathing enables you to execute multiple actions and skills at high levels of physical output. It also makes it easier for you to remember the details of the attack and the attacker.

Use your brains to outsmart bad big people by thinking before you do anything.

Never give in, and never give up. Never think anything other than that you will not let any bad big person hurt you.

Mind power is most important, and you must always tell yourself that you can and will stop the bad big person from hurting you, and never think that you can't. Always remind yourself that you will never let anyone hurt you and will never stop trying to stop them and you will get away and you will never give up.

Think WAR and make yourself WILLING ABLE READY or think I WILL WIN or WINNERS NEVER QUIT.

Use all your senses. Look, listen, and use your sense of touch and feel, feeling the ground through your boots to make sure that you have stability and that you are ready and set to go and get away.

Little soldiers, my thinking is that by now you will have lots of "what ifs" you want to ask. What if *this* happens? What if *that* happens?

Keep reading this manual and keep having your family army instructors read and explain words and meanings to you. Keep looking and listening to the big people in your family army. By doing so, your questions will most likely be answered.

If you have any questions, write them down in your little soldiers' notebook so as not to forget them.

THINGS YOU NEED TO KNOW ABOUT STOPPING A BAD BIG PERSON HURTING YOU

Always remember it is best to take away any opportunities, options or advantages that bad big people have by knowing how to identify such dangers as early as possible, preferably in advance, and by knowing how to avoid them or how to get away and stay away from them.

Sometimes a bad big person will be so sneaky that they manage to get close to you and put you in danger before you even see them. If you cannot evade and escape or get help and you are in immediate danger from a bad big person, then you need to know what to do.

If you are in a bad situation, then you need to know how to escape or counter what the bad big person is trying to do to you and how to then get away and get help. 'Counter' means taking action to stop something bad that is happening.

You need to do this as quickly and safely as possible.

The way big soldiers in the army remember things is to practice them many times until they cannot forget them and cannot get them wrong. They call this practice "basic training" and "continuation training."

FIT AND READY

Part of your planning, preparation and practice must include doing your family army P.T. Yes, that's army talk for physical training. Your family army P.T. gives you better fitness, speed, strength, stability and skills to not only outsmart but also out-move the bad big person.

The best P.T. to get you combat fit in your little soldiers' self-defence skills is to practice your escape or counter skills many times, getting faster and stronger as you get better at doing them.

'Slow is fast' as we say in army unarmed combat training. That is, the fastest way to properly meet your training goals is to work through them carefully and methodically. So, practice your skills slowly and carefully at first and only practice your skills faster and harder when you are confident.

Playing sport or trying hard in P.T. at school will help you get fitter and stronger and as such will help with your family army evasion and escape and counter actions skills training.

SAFETY IN TRAINING

WARNING: In training and practice the training target may be referred to as the human anatomy body part that would be targeted in a real-life counter action self-defence situation. Common sense safety practices must always prevail in training and all contact impact must be with soft inanimate targets or soft surfaces and never the actual enemy training person or instructor.

Always train and practice safely. You do not want to injure yourself or your family army members in training, because injuries slow down your training. Injuries also reduce your ability to execute skills when you may need them.

Do not fully straighten your stamp kicking leg in training. Also be accurate, so that you do not miss the target. This is important because either fully straightening your leg when kicking or missing the target means that you risk over-straightening your leg, which can injure you.

When you are training, you must listen carefully to everything you are being told and you must watch carefully everything you are being shown.

Remember you can always ask sensible questions of your dad, your mum or your big brothers or sisters about your basic training.

Safety for everyone who is training is very important. If you do not understand your training instructions, then be sure to ask questions until you do understand.

When your family army instructor asks you if you understand you can say "yes, instructor", "no, instructor" or "I do not understand, instructor", like a good little soldier.

Then, when you know your skills well, you can practice them more quickly. When you are told by your family army instructor that a skill you have been trying to do correctly is now being done correctly, then you can practice it until you cannot forget it and cannot get it wrong.

NEVER ABUSE OR MISUSE YOUR SKILLS

Little soldiers, always remember that self-defence is not a game.

You must use your self-defence skills only when bad big people try to hurt you.

Never use your self-defence skills on other little people, friends or your family army. These are serious skills and you must not use them for showing off, or when fooling around, or because you are angry. Practice safely by following your little soldiers safe training practices orders and instructions.

THE POWER OF POSITIVE THINKING AND BEST OPTION DECISION MAKING

Read the following carefully little soldiers and ask your family army instructor to explain anything you do not understand.

When you must get away from danger, look, decide and go. Once you make the D, that's army unarmed combat talk for *decision*, then go for it. There is no time for overthinking or worrying about whether *this* or *that* could happen. Just look, decide, think WAR "WILLING ABLE READY" and from a ready, set position go for it.

If your decided option is failing to work, use "fast mapping" (that's Todd unarmed combat systems talk for assessing and deciding on the move) to choose the best way to get and keep safe, make any adjustments and execute your decided option. You will learn other options as you work your way through this training program.

Always look for obstacles and dangers and be ready to change direction to avoid them. Sometimes you can use obstacles as barriers between you and the bad big person to make you safer and to help you stop an attack or to set up your evasion and escape.

LITTLE SOLDIERS' STANCES

Your stance, yes, the way you stand when you need to escape or protect yourself, must make you a compact, stable and ready to escape or ready to protect yourself little soldier.

Neutral Stance

Standing with your boots shoulder-width apart and your toes and heels in line gives you even, neutral footing enabling you to pivot and move diagonally forward on either side.

While you may feel uneasy about facing a bad big person, you must not show it. Setting a neutral ready stance means that you can maintain a covert ready status and not lose your element of surprise.

If the bad big person thinks you are not aware of what they are trying to do to you, then you can keep yourself safer while you decide how to escape before they can make a move.

Instructor checklist: make sure your little soldier...

- Has their toes and heels of their boots in line and shoulder-width apart.
- Prepares themselves by controlled unarmed combat breathing (inhaling through their nose and exhaling through their mouth by means of slow low-intensity cycled respiration).

Front Stance

The front stance can be used when you need to escape to the side or diagonally to your rear. It enables you to get off the mark faster and improves stability. You can discreetly change from a neutral stance to a front stance by sliding a boot straight back on the side you want to escape to.

When you slide your boot back, make sure the toes are in line with the heel of the now-front boot and that your boots are shoulder-width apart.

Slide your boot back like it is on a railway track so it stays shoulder-width apart from the other boot.

Instructor checklist: make sure your little soldier...

- Has the toes of their rear boot in line with the heel of their front boot shoulder-width apart.

- Prepares themselves by controlled unarmed combat breathing and that they maintain a discreet ready footing status.

EVASION AND ESCAPE

Immediate sprint-start run evasion and escape diagonally forward

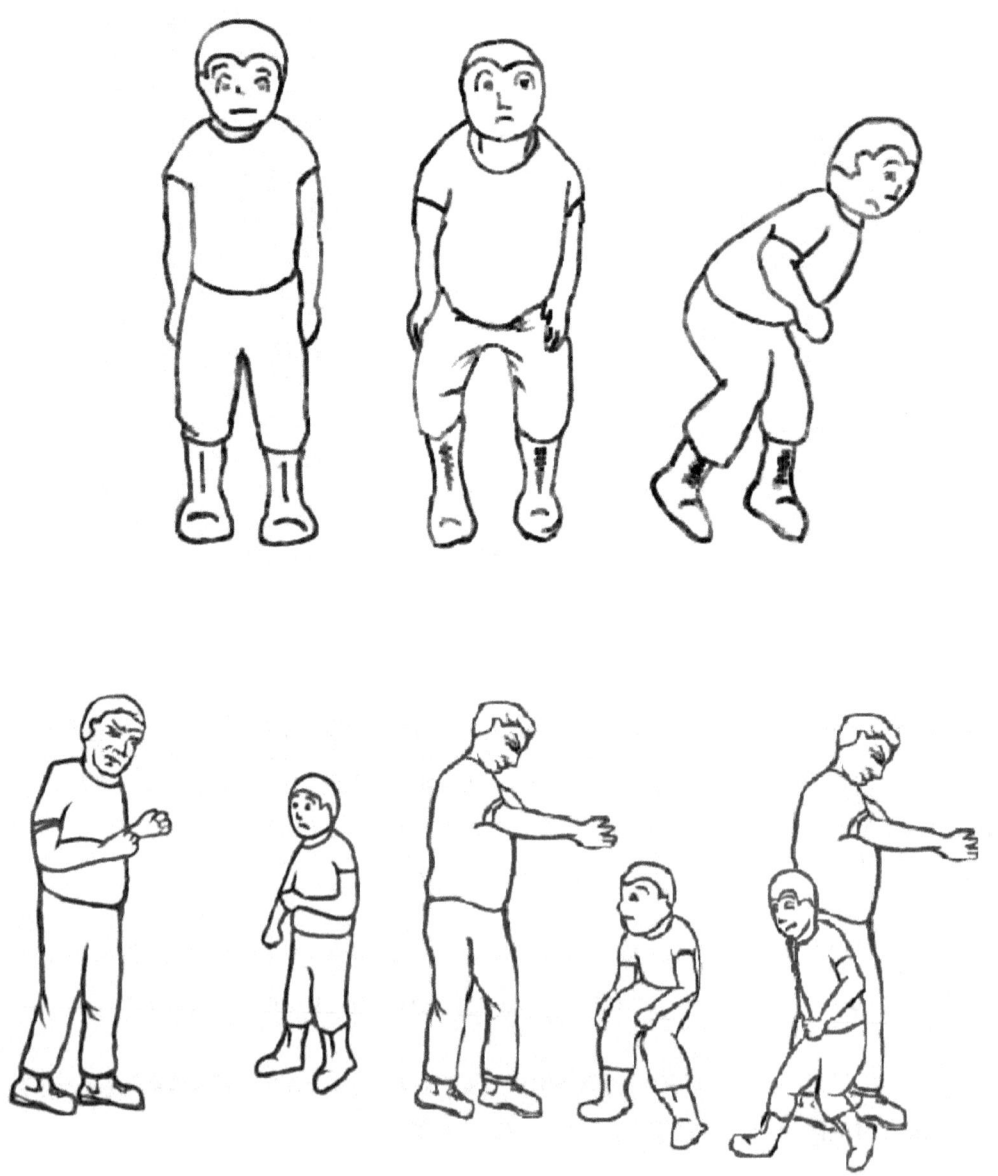

Start your diagonally forward evasion from the squat-crouch position from your neutral stance.

Pivot both boots to the left to evade diagonally forward to the left or pivot both boots to the right to evade diagonally forward to the right.

Pivot on the balls of your feet, not your heels.

From the squat-crouch position, pivot and run diagonally forward, explosively powering the kick-off movement with your rearmost boot.

Keep your arms and hands pinned to the sides of your body.

Breathe in through your nose when you squat-crouch and breathe out through your mouth when you pivot and begin your evasion.

Your army unarmed combat squat crouch and pivot ready-set-go breathing should be used to set up and kick off your sprint-start running away from danger. After this, you will need to breathe just like you do in a running race.

<u>Instructor checklist: make sure your little soldier...</u>

- Starts a diagonally forward evasion from the neutral stance from a squat-crouch position.
- Pivots both boots to the left to evade diagonally to the left.
- Pivots both boots to the right to evade diagonally to the right.
- Pivoting should be on the balls of the feet, not the heels.
- From the squat-crouch position runs diagonally forward, pushing hard off the back boot.
- Keeps arms and hands pinned to the side of the body.
- Breathes in through their nose when squat-crouching and breathes out through their mouth when pivoting and beginning the evasion.

Immediate sprint-start run evasion and escape diagonally rearward

Covertly slide your boot backwards to a front stance on the side you will evade and escape to.

Fast squat-crouch, breathe in through your nose and keep your arms to your sides and hands to your front. Breathe out through your mouth and pivot diagonally away from the bad big person to the side of your rearmost boot. Sprint-start run diagonally away from the bad big person to safety.

<u>Instructor checklist: make sure your little soldier…</u>

- Covertly slides one boot backwards to a front stance. The rear boot side is the direction your little soldier will evade and escape to.

- Fast squat-crouches and breathes in through the nose.

- Pin their arms to the side and their hands to the front of the body, to reduce the chance that their arms are grabbed.

- Breathes out through the mouth and pivots diagonally away from the bad big person.

- Your little soldier should continue to breathe out as they sprint-start run diagonally away from the bad big person.

After taking off away from the bad big person, run as fast as you can towards safety. That may mean turning around and going back rather than continuing in the direction you were first going. Know trusted local people and safe places to go to and how to get to them in quick time.

If the bad big person is chasing you, use zig-zagging to make it harder for them to catch you.

Squat-crouch and pivot both of your boots while evading to change the direction you are running in. Do this every few seconds if you need to while evading to make it as hard as possible for the bad big person to get a hold of you. Make sure your arms are pinned to your body while you evade and escape if the bad big person is chasing you and could grab hold of your arms.

While escaping and evading, make sure that you are not running blindly into hazards like cars, stationary objects or dead ends. Look in the direction you are running in and use your peripheral vision to spot hazards to your sides.

BREAKING DISTANCE TO EVADE AND ESCAPE

If faced with a frontal approach by a bad big person that is very close to you, you need to make distance to be able to sprint-run escape. So, squat-crouch and take two or three big paces backwards or pivot and take two or three big paces diagonally backwards to a front stance with your rear boot on the side you will sprint-start run away to. Immediately pivot towards your rear boot side to face diagonally away from the bad big person. Squat-crouch, inhale, exhale and then sprint-run escape.

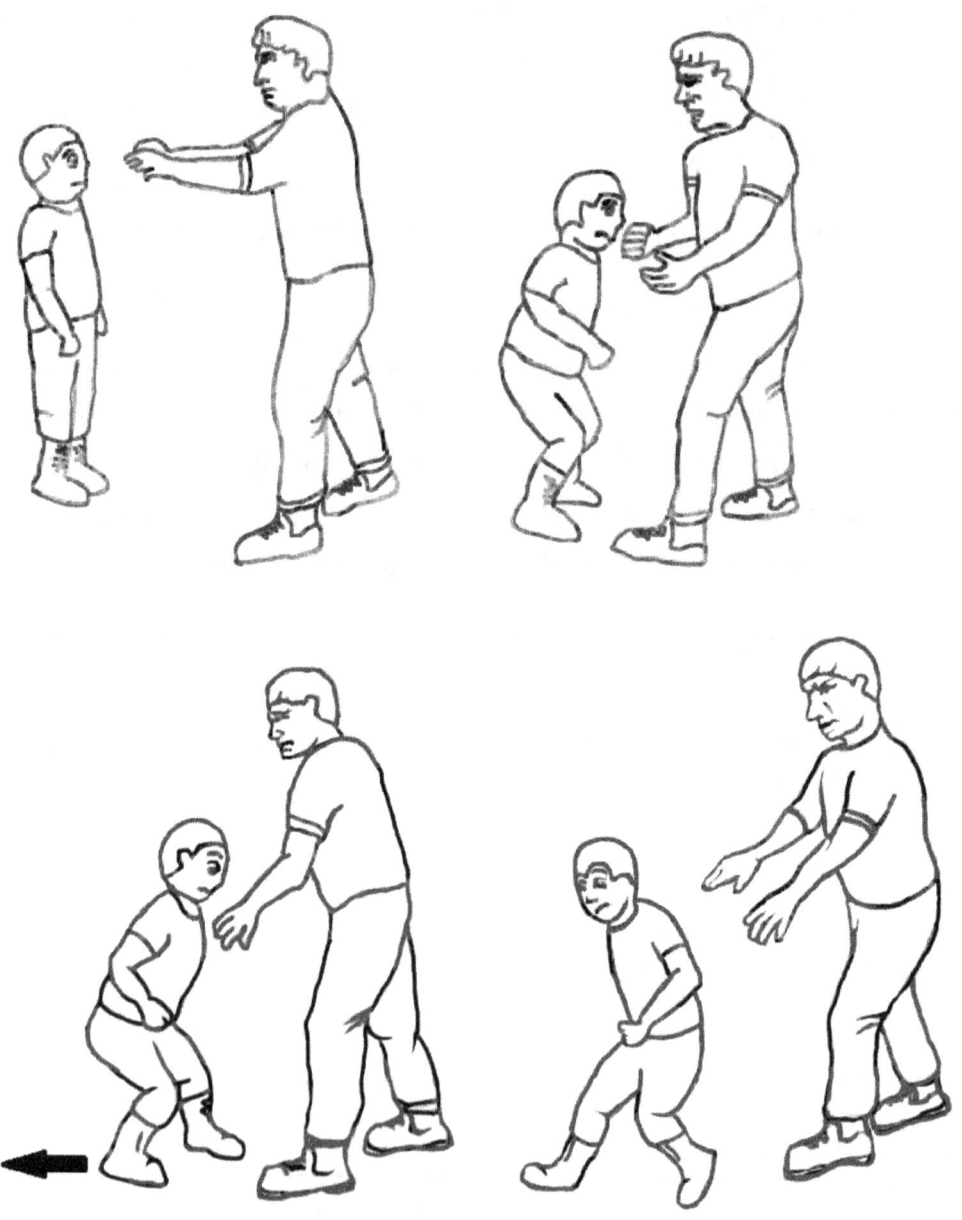

Instructor checklist: make sure your little soldier...

- Squat-crouches and takes two or three big paces backwards or pivots and takes two or three big steps diagonally backwards to a front stance. Your little soldier's rearmost boot is the side they will sprint-start run away to.

- Quickly inhales, squat-crouches, exhales, pivots to the rearmost boot side to face away from the bad big person.

- Continues exhaling and sprint-start run escapes.

Instruct your little soldier that after getting back two or three paces' distance in the decided direction, they must sprint-start run between five and ten metres. This is excellent sprint-start run evasion and escape initiation and execution practice.

Practice breaking distance from the training enemy bad big person directly and diagonally rearward and then sprint-start run escape to both sides.

All movement execution actions should be employed from an initial squat-crouch pivot status with synchronised breathing.

When your little soldiers can break a safe range from you, their training enemy bad big person, give them varied directions of escape and have them evade and escape as per your instructions. When they can evade and escape as per your instructions and directions without getting it wrong, increase the sprint-start run distances and have them zig-zag by pivoting and changing direction on the move to avoid being seized or by squat-crouching, pivoting and zig zagging if in immediate arms' reach of being grabbed.

Family army instructor, your role as the enemy training party is to train your little soldier to best escape a bad big person. This is best done for learning purposes by utilising a "less is more" approach (that is, economy of movement is preferred) and remembering that "slow is fast" (that is, the fastest way to properly meet your training goals is to work through them carefully and methodically).

So have your little soldier practice one individual skill at a time in parts slowly and then in full slowly.

Be sure they fully understand what the skill is to be used for and how to execute it.

Give them scenarios as to danger areas that they need to avoid and directions of escape they need to take so that they learn to assess and decide on directions based on getting away from the threat and avoiding any hazards. This helps them to head in the best evasion and escape directions.

Set places of safety they need to head towards when training.

Only when they cannot get it wrong should you increase the speed and take up the role of the bad big person chasing them.

For zig-zag evasion and escape practice, instruct your little soldier to silently count in their head 1... 2... 3 as they are running and to then change direction.

During the learning and practice phases of training, as you chase your little soldier, instruct them how to keep out of arms' reach by increasing their run speed and by executing zig-zagging changes of direction.

To prevent being grabbed on the run instruct them to change direction by squat-crouching and pivoting with every direction change.

Let your little soldier know that you will lightly tag them to indicate they have been caught by you, their practice enemy bad big person.

Later in this training manual, tactics and skills will be provided on what to do if your little soldier has been seized and secured and cannot get away. However, the focus initially must be on the primary practice of evasion and escape.

LITTLE SOLDIERS HIT THE DECK: ARMY UNARMED CQC SIDE FALL

This lesson is about how to safely fall to the ground the army unarmed combat way. The safe way to fall is called a 'CQC side fall' (CQC is abbreviated army talk for close quarters combat).

Side falling is very important if you cannot get away to stop being abducted.

Some of you may not be fast runners, and to stop being abducted you might have to get to the ground and counter stamp kick (as described later in this manual) as part of your side fall or from the ground after side falling to prevent being abducted.

Side falling to the ground can make you hard to get hold of or keep hold of.

Side falling is also important if you fall, trip, or are pushed or knocked to the ground because it can prevent or reduce injury.

To execute a side fall, you must squat as low as you can, very close to kneeling, but be careful not to injure your kneecaps on the ground. Now pivot both your boots in the direction you want to fall to and bend your body forward and downward to your thighs. Keep your hands on the back of your neck with your palms and fingers protecting the back of your head and neck and your forearms and elbows locked tight inside your thighs (this is called a "cover guard" or a "hard cover guard"). Keep your face inside your forearms. You need to get into a tight foetal position making yourself curved and compact to reduce hard full body contact impact with the ground.

As you fall and make contact with the ground, rock backwards and away from the bad big person then forward to reduce ground impact.

Your ground contact when side falling will be a rocking action from the outside of your boot along the outside of your leg to the outside of your buttock and up to the outside of your upper arm as you fall down and away from the bad big person. This will spread the impact up one side of your compressed, curved body line. Ground contact must be with the side of your body and never your spine, neck, head or top of your shoulder joint. Breathe out as you fall to reduce the chances of getting winded when you contact with the ground.

The army CQC side fall can be executed in any direction: forwards, to the side or to your rear flanks (that's unarmed combat talk for behind you).

You can fall towards any hour on the clock, and you should practice doing so (12 o'clock is in front centre of you, three o'clock is to your right, six o'clock is behind you, and nine o'clock is to your left).

You need to always make sure that the direction you will fall is safe. Assess, squat-crouch, cover guard to protect the back of your head and neck, pivot in the direction you want to fall and make sure that direction is away from the bad big person. Be sure to breathe in as you squat crouch and breathe out as you pivot and fall from as low to the ground as possible in a rocking motion.

Always fall away from the bad big person so that your head is away from them and your boots are towards them.

You have an advantage over the bad big person: You are smaller and nimbler than they are, making you hard to grab hold of. So, use this advantage to make yourself a small, compact, hard and fast target in escaping, stamp kicking and escaping or if you can't escape or stamp kick and escape, by side falling to counter their grab.

If you have to go to the ground to prevent the bad big person getting hold of you, squat-crouch groundward fast like a dead weight and then pivot away from the bad big person and safely CQC side fall.

Remember: if you have to fall to the ground, breathe out as you fall, inhale through your nose as you squat-crouch, put on your hard cover guard, pivot and breathe out through your mouth as you safely fall from as low to the ground as possible, falling away from the bad big person.

Be as hard to get hold of, keep hold of, lift or move as you can be. I reiterate, breathe in, squat-crouch, drop your weight hard and fast to as low of a squat-crouch as possible, put your hard cover guard on to protect the back of your head and neck, breathe out, pivot and fall groundward down and away from the bad big person. If you can break free, then recover your footing and sprint-start run away getting away to safety. After this, getting help is the priority.

Instructor checklist. Make sure your little soldier…

- Squats as low as they can to almost kneeling. Be careful not to let them injure their knees on the ground.

- Pivots both boots to the side they want to fall on.

- Bends their body forwards and downwards to their thighs.

- Keeps their hands on the back of their neck. Their fingers and palms will protect the back of their neck and head.

- Locks their forearms and elbows tight inside their thighs.

- Keeps their face inside their forearms.

- Curls up tight like a ball to prevent hitting the ground hard.

- When they fall on the ground they rock backwards and away from the bad big person then forwards. This prevents them from getting hurt when falling, by minimising impact with the ground.

- Makes ground contact by rocking from their boot, along their leg, to the side of their buttock, to the outside of their upper arm and just inside the shoulder blade as they fall down and away from the bad big person. This helps prevent injury from the fall.

- Falls on the side of their body, never on their back, neck, head or the top of their shoulder.

- Breathes in through their nose as part of the side fall set up and breathes out through their mouth on the pivot and side falling action.

Escaping should always be the first option for your little soldier. If they cannot immediately sprint-run evade and escape the bad big person, then make sure your little soldier knows that they can stamp kick and sprint-run escape to safety and as a last resort can ground side fall away from the bad big person.

It is important that they know what option to use in order of effectiveness and safety and you provide practice in all options.

1. Immediate sprint run evade and escape.

2. Stamp-kick and sprint run escape.

3. Ground side fall and footing recover escape.

FOOTING RECOVERY

You need to use a tactical footing recovery method after side falling, or from any other ground position. This puts you into a position to sprint-start run away or to stand up.

If you are already on your side, then you are ready to recover your footing. If you are not already on your side, then roll onto your side.

Once you are on your side, bend your upper leg at the knee and move it forward, over your lower leg until your upper leg's knee is on the ground.

Put the palm and forearm of your lower hand and arm on the ground. Place the palm of your upper hand on the ground forward of it. Push up to kneeling on both knees and then place the sole of one boot on the ground. Pivot on your knee and boot to face the direction you want to sprint-start away in.

Get into a sprint-start ready position and sprint-start run away.

To recover your footing to end up in a standing position, come up to a kneeling on one knee position and stand up.

Instructor checklist: make sure your little soldier...

- Starts their footing recovery from side on.
- Places their upper leg over their lower leg and bends their upper knee, bringing it into contact with the ground.
- Places their lower palm and forearm on the ground and places their upper hand on the ground in front of it.
- Pushes up to kneeling then places the sole of one boot on the ground.
- Pivots on the ground in the direction of escape and breathes in.
- Breathes out as they sprint-start run escape.

STAMP KICKS

Stamp kicking is the safest, hardest and most powerful counter measure your little soldier can produce. I will discuss stamp kicking and then give detailed instruction for each type of stamp kick.

Family army instructor, make sure that your little soldier learns and practices all stamp kicks slowly, correctly and carefully initially.

Make sure they do not hyperextend their kicking leg and that they keep their foot, ankle and lower leg joints in line just like they are in a natural footing stationary standing position.

Make sure your little soldier contacts the target with the arch of their boot, so that the sole of their boot between the heel and the ball of their foot encapsulates the target in training. The target is the shin of the bad big person in real life stamp kick self-protection executions.

When stamp kicking from a standing position, one boot remains on the ground for stability. This ground-stability boot will be pointing with the toe away from the target, and the stamp kicking boot will be horizontally in line with and closest to the target in training.

The stamp kick for soldiers in the army is often employed offensively as an entry assault towards the enemy or from point blank body contact range with the enemy.

The aim for the soldier is, from stationary, to destroy the integrity of the knee joint or kneecap and as such the ligaments that hold the joint and cap in place.

There are a range of stamp kicking options for soldiers in military CQC, but for your little soldiers' self-protection, the stamp kick needs to fit the threat specifics and your little soldiers' capabilities and limitations.

Stamp kicks are the primary unarmed offensive assault in military unarmed self-defence. They have commonality across multiple different threats for your little soldiers.

Nothing is guaranteed under threat and the risk increases considerably in threats against children by bad big people.

Your little soldiers do not have the physical size and attributes needed to employ all the stamp kicks used by soldiers in the army. So, the stamp kicks selected for your little soldiers' training program have been chosen to maximise safety and effectiveness in achieving outcomes. The goal of stamp kicking to the lower leg is to stop the attack, enable evasion and escape, or buy time until a good big person can come to their aid. Stamp kicking can make your little soldier a hard target. The stamp kick may incapacitate a bad big person or keep them at bay, decentralize them (that is, physically unbalance them), reduce the chance that they can quickly seize and secure your little soldiers, and increase the chances of the bad big person being caught.

For example, if lying on the ground, stamp kicking the fingers or thumb of a bad big person's hand that is grasping a little soldier's limb can cause a quick release of their grip.

For your little soldiers, the primary stamp kick executions will be from stationary to prevent the bad big person getting close to them, getting hold of them or abducting them. Threat specifics in child abduction require little soldiers to be able to resist forward pulling forced movement by resisting and sliding towards, or if being pushed, resisting and sliding away from the bad big person and setting up stamp kicks from a standing squat-crouch, kneeling or lying down on the ground position. Each of these will be discussed in detail in this manual.

Stamp kicks are increased in safety and effectiveness by your little soldier squat-crouching fast, low and hard, and by pivoting away from the bad big person.

Unlike soldiers in the army, your little soldiers will not need to cover ground towards the threat, as getting away is their priority. So, stamp kicks will be executed from stationary or, if seized by the bad big person, under forced sliding resistance.

Your little soldiers may have to make close to point-blank range footing adjustments to best set up their stamp kicks.

Squat-crouching down and pivoting away from the bad big person as part of setting up and executing stamp kicks for counter abduction will make your little soldier a much harder target. Proper breathing will increase their capabilities. Always inhale via the nose on the set up and exhale via the mouth on the execution.

Side falling to maximise prevention or resistance against abduction and ground stamp kicking will provide a last line of defence to counter an abduction attempt.

Family army instructor, you need to keep your stamp kicking instruction simple and ensure your little soldier understands and can execute stamp kicks from the squat-crouch, from kneeling and when lying on the ground.

You need to check and ensure that your little soldier knows their correct range to maximise stamp kicking effect. They also need to know how to adjust footing and body position to set up the best stamp kicks they can. Counter abduction resistance training must provide capability to prevent abduction by resistance which is achieved by low fast hard squat-crouching combined with pivoting away from the bad big person.

Under forced abduction, when the bad big person is overpowering your little soldier and forcibly moving them, yielding by controlled resistance sliding towards or away from the bad big person and point-blank boot-to-boot contact range stamp kicking is a last line of defence in stopping the abduction.

The stamp kicks are as simple and safe as self-defence gets and have commonality across multiple threats. You must ensure that your little soldiers practice them until they can't get them wrong.

Read your little soldiers stamp kick instructions and look carefully at the diagrams. Practice them yourself so that you can demonstrate and instruct them with confidence and competence.

PRACTICING LEG STAMPS SAFELY

Your little soldiers' stamp kicks need to be practiced safely, without injuring the instructor or themselves. This can be achieved by careful use of a bag, pad or an old soft-compound car tyre.

Family army instructors must protect themselves against injury by ensuring that the base of the stamp kicking bag is securely positioned on the ground with the stamp kicking bag leaning diagonally backwards towards the holder, and with the instructor's legs well out of danger.

Alternatively, the bag can be laid horizontally flat on the ground and can be braced against your thighs if you are kneeling. Then your little soldier can stamp kick the front top of the bag closest to themselves.

If you chose to kneel and hold the bag upright, lean it diagonally towards yourself with the base edge pushed away from you and placed firmly onto the ground surface.

When standing or kneeling, always hold the bag diagonally up and away from your little soldier and make sure it is kept firmly in position and that your hands, legs and any other part of your anatomy are safely away from contact.

Bags or pads positioned flat on the ground can also be placed against a robust solid backdrop. Similarly, a soft-compound car tyre can be screwed or bolted upright to a wooden fence post or tree trunk. You can also bury the upright car tyre half in the ground.

Alternatively, you can kneel on one knee and brace the back of the tyre against your thigh with one side of the tyre against the inner thigh of your forward leg, or you can kneel down on both knees with the back of the tyre secured against one or both thighs. Secure the tyre with both hands at the top or back of the tyre, locking it firmly and securely in position. Make sure your legs, feet and hands are well clear of any possible accidental impact.

You can use chalk, paint or tape on the target at or below adult knee height for a target reference for your little soldier.

To protect your little soldiers against ankle, foot or lower leg injuries when learning and practicing, make sure that their stamp kicking boot is in contact or close to being in contact with the front of the impact target prior to executing the stamp kick. This ensures that their stamp kicks are executed from a safe and effective range.

Make sure their boots and legs are in the correct alignment position. The stamp kicking boot should be at a right angle to the target and the rear stability boot should be pointing directly away from the target. Instruct your little soldier and make sure that they do not hyperextend their stamp kicking leg. A range adjustment may be needed to avoid hyperextension.

Have clear family army rules that include when and with whom your little soldiers can train. This will reduce the likelihood of injuries outside of family army training.

If you allow them to practice on a static impact stamp kicking target like a half-buried car tyre, then they must know how to safely practice to prevent self-injury. Your little soldiers must not train in the presence of non-family army members. Similarly, they must not show their skills to other children who have not been trained in these skills and that do not have their parents' and your permission.

Unsupervised practice is not recommended, but if you do allow it then there must be stringent rules.

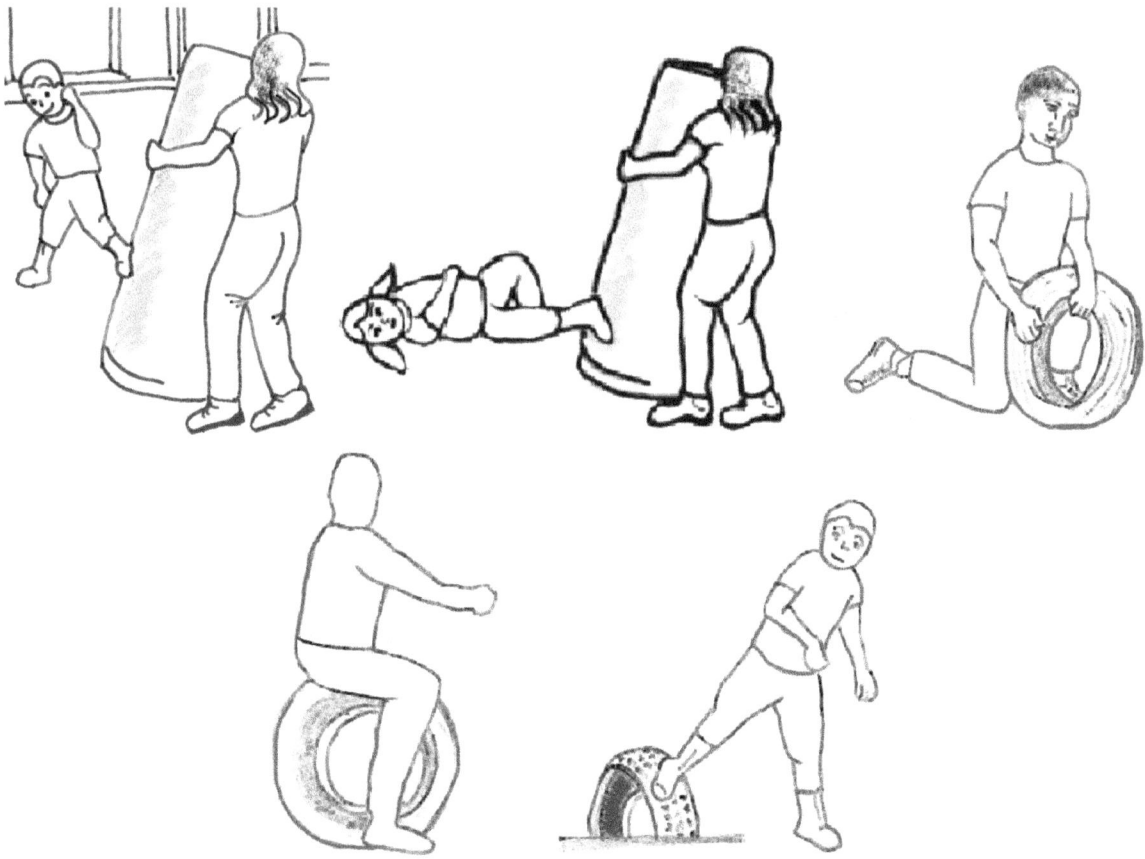

Examples of training equipment being used to practice leg stamps safely.

Little soldiers, you can have your family army instructor half bury an old car tyre in the ground to use as your stamp kicking target. Your family army instructor should choose a tyre that is not too hard. Your instructor knows how to set up indoors and outdoors stamp kick targets for you.

Always kick low and accurately and never kick your family army instructor's hands holding the tyre or their legs or feet or any of their body parts.

Employ your army unarmed combat breathing with every stamp kick executed. Breathe in through your nose as you squat-crouch and set up the stamp kick and breathe out through your mouth as you pivot and execute the stamp kick.

If you need to make more footing adjustments after inhaling through your nose but before exhaling through your mouth and executing the stamp kick, just exhale and inhale and exhale again as you stamp kick.

Once you can execute the stamp kick without error, increase the speed and commitment of the kick.

You can practice multiple stamp kicks by adjusting your footing and range between each stamp kick to ensure your stamp kicking boot is in contact range with the target and your stance and footing are correct.

When you feel you can safely execute the stamp kick hard and fast, try to stamp kick right down through the target, but remember never to fully straighten your leg as you could injure yourself. If you feel like you need to fully straighten your leg when you stamp kick this is a sign that you are not close enough to the target.

Imagine the sides of your stamp kicking target as the outsides of a bad big person's lower leg and stamp kick from outside the target diagonally downward. Always practice skills in parts and then in full. Begin slowly. Increase speed and power only after you can safely execute the skill without error.

When making adjustments, pivot and slide your boots but do not lift them off of the ground. This skill will come only after practicing a number of stamp kicks so that you get to feel that your set up positioning and execution feels safe and stable and you can execute your stamp kick with speed, power and stability.

Every second that the bad big person cannot get hold of you, pick you up or drag you away counts in your favour. Every second of trouble you give them makes you a harder target and too much of a problem. Your actions could make the bad big person think that they are going to fail, get caught, and go to jail and as a result they may decide to stop attacking you and run away.

By your actions you are making yourself a hard and difficult target. When you combine this with yelling "help me, get the police!, please help me!," to raise the alarm, there is a good chance that good big people will come to your rescue. This means that the bad big person will have to run away and/or will get caught and get taken to jail.

You need to practice your self-defence stamp kick from several different positions. You should practice the stamp kick from a standing crouched position, from a
kneeling down position, and from a lying down on the ground position. You will learn all these variations of stamp kicks in this manual. You need to get your dad, mum, or big brother or sister family army instructors to hold your stamp kick bag correctly and safely.

Tackle bags, cushions and tyres can all be used to practice leg stamps safely.

Training is important and you need to do lots of training and practice to be the best little family army soldier you can be. That is exactly what big soldiers in the army do.

You need to practice by using your big family members as instructors. Sometimes your instructors can play the part of the bad big person. For example, suppose that you want to practice kicking from the ground to stop a bad big person dragging you away. Suppose that the bad big person is dragging you by the wrist or wrists. To practice countering this, your family army instructor can kneel down with the stamp kick bag flat on the ground in front of and firmly against their thighs, they can hold your wrist or wrists, and then you can fall away from your "enemy per" (that's army talk for a bad big person in training) to the ground by side falling commando style, and you can stamp kick the stamp-kick bag.

When you have broken their hold on your wrist or wrists, regain your footing and sprint off, or barrel roll away out of reach of the bad big person, and then recover your footing and sprint away.

Your practice can also be done using a half-buried tyre with your family army instructor sitting on and straddling the tyre and playing the part of the enemy per.

Family army instructors, point out that the stamp kick must be below the height of a bad big person's knee joint and never above the knee joint.

The stamp kick must make contact below the kneecap. A slightly low stamp kick is better than one that is too high.

Initially practice skills in these components until your little soldiers can execute skills in one cohesive action: inhale, squat-crouch, exhale, pivot, adjust-footing, stamp-kick.

A stamp kick practiced in many parts can be reduced by one part at a time as your little soldier gains competency in the previous parts. Eventually the entire kick will be practiced in one fluid action.

Start off with 10 repetitions of each skill practiced initially in parts and then in full. Make sure to take at least 10 seconds' non-action time between each repetition during the learning phase of training. Stamp kicks are deliberate definite actions that require skill, accuracy and commitment. To maintain maximum physical capabilities, should multiple counter stamp kicks executions be required, each stamp should be set up and any adjustments made in range and position to maximise stability and effectiveness.

Every stamp kick is executed as if your little soldier's safety depends upon it. Range, stance, position, adjustment, breathing, skill, commitment and accuracy should all be combined to maximise velocity. This is what your little soldier is training to achieve.

When practicing stamp kicks, the range is very important. If you pause to check range, your little soldier's stamp kicking boot should be able to touch or almost touch the target before the kick is executed. This range achieves the best destructive power. Stamp kicking out of range, however, increases the risks of injury and failure.

Timing and range are very important. If the bad big person is closing in on your little soldier, it is important that they time their stamp kick so they execute it when the bad big person is in full stamp kicking contact range. This may require an adjustment in position or moving off the line of the incoming bad big person prior to stamp kicking.

If they have been seized and are being dragged towards the bad big person, they will most likely find that they are sliding towards them. It is important that they resist the forced movement by pivoting and leaning away from the bad big person and pushing into the ground away from the bad big person's forced movement with the soles of their boots.

When they are in maximum impact contact range, and not before, they should execute their stamp kick or kicks. Under such forced movements, they can execute their kicks from kneeling or lying down on the ground, to increase resistance and hard targeting, to prevent abduction.

Your little soldiers can never be too close to execute a stamp kick, but if they stamp kick from too far away, their stamp kick can fall short of the target, and they will lose the element of surprise. This increases the risk of being abducted.

They can effectively stamp kick hard from boot-to-boot contact with the bad big person whether they are standing, kneeling or lying down on the ground.

Close range for your little soldier to stamp kick would be approximately 10 cm or less from your little soldiers' stamp kicking boot to the bad big person's closest leg to them. Effective ranges to maximise impact contact are from 10cm or closer to the target, right up to boot-to-boot contact range.

Initially your little soldier should practice stamp kicks from side on to the target.

Once your little soldier has learnt to execute a side-on-to-the-target stamp kick (both boots and the target are in line) and can execute it correctly every time, they can move into a side-on-to-the-target front stance stamp kick. If the target leg is in front of your little soldier, they will slide their stability boot directly forward to a side on front stance.

If the target leg is behind your little soldier they will slide the stability boot backwards to a side-on front stance.

The side-on-to-the-target front stance provides increased stability and outer target leg alignment and is a simple stability boot transition from a side stance.

Both the side-on stance and the side-on front stance provide simple stamp kicking effectiveness and safety.

Their body being side on fits well with squat-crouching, pivoting and leaning away from the bad big person, making them harder to seize and secure.

STAMP KICK TO THE SIDE

To execute a standing stamp kick when you are side on to the target, position your stamp kicking boot arch against the bad big person's target leg's toes.

Breathe in through your nose as you squat-crouch, then pivot your toes away from the target and raise your stamp kicking boot and leg and look down at the target as you breathe out through your mouth and stamp kick the target.

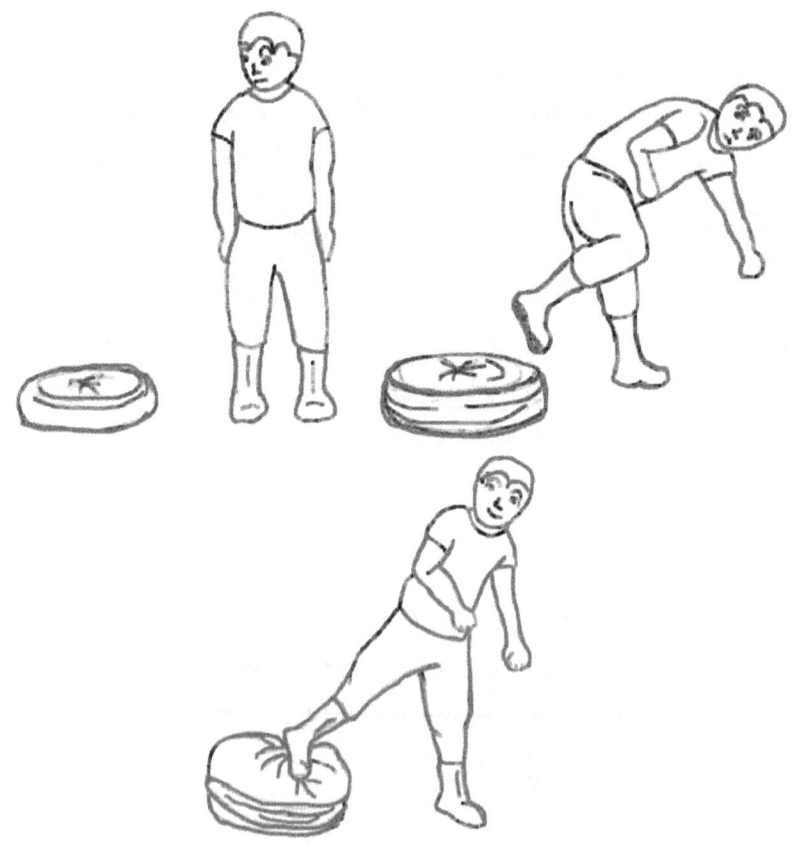

Instructor checklist: make sure your little soldier…

- Is in the correct stamp kicking range.

- Has their stamp kicking boot arch positioned next to the bad big person's target leg's toes.

- Squat-crouches and breathes in.

- Breathes out, pivots their toes away from the target, raises the stamp kicking leg, looks down at the target and stamp kicks the target.

STAMP KICK FROM A SIDE-ON FRONT STANCE

Move your stamp kicking boot in against or close to your target and make any footing adjustments. Slide your stability boot (that is, the boot that is furthest from the target in a straight line) either forward or backwards to a side-on front stance. The reason for sliding your stability boot forward or backwards is to position yourself to be able to stamp kick from the outside of the bad big person's lower leg/target. This is very important if you must stop a bad big person from being able to harm you. Stamp kicking the bad big person's closest lower leg to your stamp kicking boot from the outside of the target leg increases your chances of stopping them from getting hold of you and makes them fall away from you.

If you need more adjustment to line your stamping boot up to the target (after sliding your stability boot in a straight line forward or backward to get outside the target leg), you can make minor footing adjustments including pivoting and sliding to get into position.

To make the decision as to if you should slide your rear boot forward or backward to get outside the bad big person's front boot, undertake the following
assessment: if their front leg is in front of you, slide your rear boot forward and if their front leg is behind you, slide your rear leg boot backwards.

If you cannot stamp kick from outside their closest leg, stamp kick to the front of their closest lower leg. Breathe in through your nose as you squat-crouch, breathe out through your mouth as you pivot both your boots away from the target, look at the target, raise your stamp-kicking leg and boot and stamp kick diagonally right through the target to the ground.

Instructor checklist: make sure your little soldier...

- Moves their stamp kicking boot against or close to the target.
- Slides their furthest boot forwards or backwards to a side on front stance.
- Pivots their boots diagonally away from the target leg to a stamp kick position.
- Breathes in and squat crouches.
- Breathes out, pivots and leg stamps outside of the kick target below knee height.

To help your little soldier decide whether to slide their furthest away leg forwards or backwards remember: If the bad big person's closest leg is in-line or in front of their stamp kicking boot, slide their furthest away boot forward. If the bad big person's closest leg is in-line or behind their stamp kicking boot slide their furthest away boot backwards. Their stability boot needs to be outside the kicking target.

STAMP KICK TO YOUR REAR FLANKS

To stamp kick a bad big person to your rear flanks, slide the boot of your non-stamp-kicking stability leg directly forward and away from the target, so that you are in a front stance.

Then, pivot both your boots slightly diagonally forward to your stamp kicking boot side while looking over your shoulder to set a diagonal front stance. Make any footing adjustments to get into range and for safety and stability.

Breathe in through your nose as you squat-crouch. Breathe out through your mouth as you raise the boot closest to the target leg and stamp kick with the arch of the sole of that boot.

<u>Instructor checklist: make sure your little soldier...</u>

- Slides their non-kicking boot forward, away from the target, into a front stance.

- Pivots both boots slightly to the stamp kicking boot side while looking over their shoulder to see the target.

- Makes adjustments when required for range and stability.

- Squat-crouches and breathes in through their nose.

- Breathes out through their mouth as they stamp kick with the arch of the sole of the boot to the closest target leg.

LEAD LEG STAMP KICK TO THE FRONT FROM FRONT STANCE

To execute a lead-leg stamp kick to the front, position yourself in a front stance with your lead stamp-kicking boot on the ground in contact or close to being in contact with the target leg of the bad big person. Breathe in through your nose as you squat-crouch and breathe out through your mouth as you pivot both your boots rearwards away from the target towards your rear boot. Raise your lead stamp kicking boot leg and stamp kick the targeted closest leg of the bad big person.

Instructor checklist: make sure your little soldier...

- Positions themselves in a front stance, placing their kicking leg in contact or close to the target leg of the bad big person.

- Breathes in through their nose as they squat-crouch.

- Breathes out and pivots both boots slightly to their rear leg side.

- Raises the leg stamping leg as they stamp kick the closest target leg.

TOE-OF-BOOT SPIKE KICKING

Little soldier, if you cannot get into a position to stamp kick to break a bad big person's hold on you, you might be able to toe spike kick them instead to make them let go or loosen their hold on you. A toe spike kick to their ankle joint or low on the front of their shin can be very effective.

This is the type of kick Dads and Mums might have told their children not to do to their brothers or sisters.

From close to the target with your kicking boot touching the target inhale, squat-crouch and slide your kicking boot backwards away from the target then exhale and toe spike kick the target at ankle height.

You are aiming for the ball joint of the ankle or low down on the front of the shin. You can now stamp kick the target or toe spike kick the target again and then stamp kick the target and sprint-run escape.

Listen to your family army instructor and only kick slowly and softly until you know what it feels like and know you will not injure your toes, foot or ankle.

The toe of the boot spike kicking can be used for making a bad big person let go of their hold on your little soldier if they cannot stamp kick.

It may be used to set up a stamp kick by making the bad big person release their grip or hold of your little soldier so they can set up their stamp kick so they can escape to safety.

You need to be sure that your little soldier does not injure their toes, foot or ankle in training. To do so make sure that they are wearing solid footwear, the spike kicking target is soft and that they kick initially slowly at low intensity and only gradually increase the momentum contact impact in a safe manner.

From standing in front of the target in boot contact range, squat-crouch and inhale, slide the kicking boot backwards away from the target, then like kicking a football exhale and toe spike kick the target at ankle joint height. Kicking the ball joint of the ankle will cause pain and possible disengagement and release of the hold.

The front of the shin just above the ankle joint can be targeted if the ankle ball joint cannot.

The toe spike kick can be repeated by sliding a boot back and kicking again or kicking with the opposite boot.

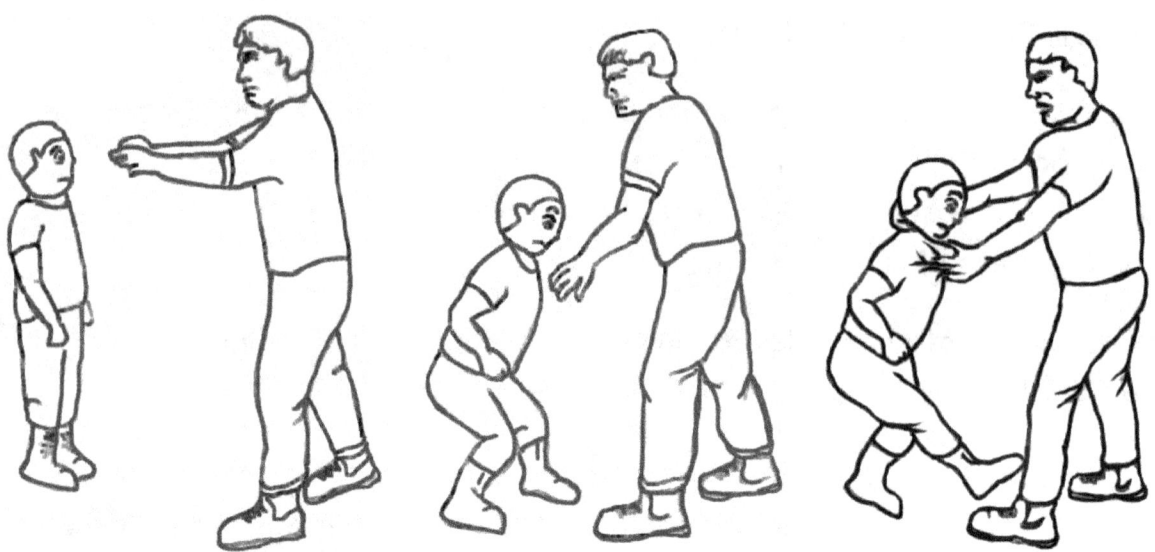

Instructor checklist: make sure your little soldier...

- Inhales, squat-crouches, slides the kicking boot backwards and away from the target.

- Exhales and low toe spike kicks the target, like kicking a football.

- Stamp kicks and escapes.

- Or repeats the toe spike kick again then stamp kicks and escapes.

STAMP KICKING FROM A KNEELING POSITION

Standing sprint-start running evasion and escape is a preventative better and safer option over seizure counter escape options.

Kneeling stamp kicking combined with a sprint-start run evasion and escape may be a required contingency option to prevent being grabbed or break a bad big persons' hold during a sprint-start run evasion and escape.

Either a preventative sprint-start run evasion and escape or a side ground fall combined with ground stamp kicks are the primary options to prevent abduction.

In situations like from a sprint-start run position where a stamp kick is required to prevent being grabbed hold of, it is a primary contingency preventative option.

Stamp kicks can be applied from a sprint-start run position with the palms of both hands on the ground, and from kneeling on one knee or both knees. Alternatively, both forearms or one forearm and the palm of one hand can be in contact with the ground.

For practice purposes start with your boots closest to the stamp kicking target kneeling on both knees facing away from the target.

Set your low, stable, close-to-the-ground kneeling position and hand/hands forearm/forearms or a combination of a forearm and hand ground contact position.

Make sure you are in stamp kicking range, breathe in through your nose, pivot to the side of the boot you will stamp kick with and make sure you are in a low, stable, kneeling position. Look backwards towards the target, either over your shoulder or under your armpit at the bad big person's target leg.

Raise your stamp kicking leg's knee and boot off of the ground and breathe out as you stamp kick the bad big person's leg.

Sprint-start run evade and escape to safety or stamp kick again and sprint-start run evade and escape to safety.

Instructor checklist: make sure your little soldier...

- Kneels on both knees at close range to the target.

- Breathes in through their nose as they pivot on their knees to the same side as their stamp kicking boot.

- Keeps low and stable, places palm/palms or forearm/forearms/one palm/one forearm on the ground to the front and looks under their armpit or over their shoulder at the target.

- Raises their closest stamp kicking knee lower leg and boot off of the ground and breathes out as they stamp kick the target.

- Sets a sprint-run start evasion and escape position and sprint-start run evades and escapes.

STATIONARY GROUND STAMP KICK

A ground leg-stamp kick is executed from lying on the ground on your side in front of the bad big person. When falling, your knees will be bent with your legs tucked up towards your body and body bent towards your thighs. After falling, your skyward closest stamp kicking leg should be above your groundward closest ground contact leg. The sole of your top leg boot will be flat on the ground and your bottom leg sole of your boot will be both on the ground and against your top boot. This is for stability and ease of ground adjustment and movement.

Make adjustments to position yourself close to the stamp-kicking target leg. Inhale through your nose as you retract and raise your skyward closest stamp kicking boot and breathe out through your mouth as you stamp kick the target leg. Focus on contacting the target leg with the arch of the sole of your boot.

Ground leg stamps can be used as part of the side falling action or when already on the ground.

Side fall, and then stamp kick immediately after side falling as part of the ground contact rocking action away from the bad big person and back towards them. This provides both safety in hitting the deck abduction prevention and also an effective stamp kicking counter action to enable footing recovery and evasion and escape.

The side fall must always be executed from as low to the ground as possible by a squat-crouching, pivoting, falling and rocking action.

Instructor checklist: make sure your little soldier...

- Starts in the post side fall position with their knees tucked up to their body and body over their thighs.
- Has their top skyward leg above their bottom groundward leg.
- Keeps their bottom leg bent and in ground contact. Make sure they are within stamp kicking range before executing the stamp kick.
- Breathes in through their nose as they pull their kicking knee in and raise their kicking boot.
- Breathes out through their mouth as they stamp kick the target.
- Encapsulates the target with the arch of the sole of their boot.

GROUND OBLIQUE STAMP KICK

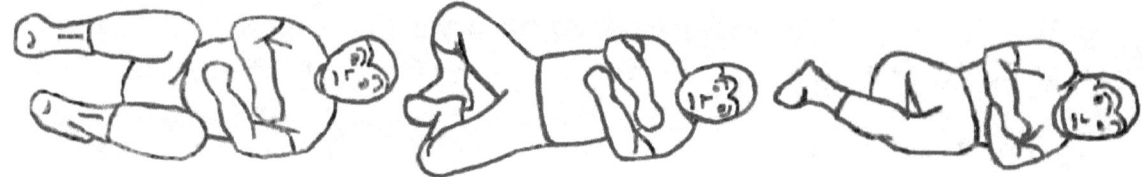

A ground oblique stamp kick is executed from lying on the ground on your side with your legs and boots as previous.

Retract and raise your ground contact leg as you inhale via your nose. Adjust the toe of your stamp-kicking bottom boot so it points diagonally outward as you breathe out via your mouth and stamp kick with the arch of the sole of your boot at the stamp-kicking target leg.

<u>Instructor checklist: make sure your little soldier...</u>

- Starts the kick lying on their side with their legs facing the bad big person and their knees bent towards their body.

- Places their top boot sole flat on ground, bottom boot sole on ground against top boot and is within stamp kicking range.

- Pulls back their bottom kicking leg as they breathe in through their nose.

- Adjusts the toe of their kicking boot so it is pointing diagonally outwards.

- Breathes out through their mouth as they stamp kick the target, encapsulating the target with the arch of the sole of the kicking boot.

GROUND LEG STAMP KICK AND OBLIQUE STAMP KICK

From lying on your side close to the bad big person's target closest leg, tuck your legs up close to your body, top leg boot sole flat on ground, bottom leg boot sole on ground and against top boot. Breathe in through your nose as you retract and lift your skyward leg and breathe out through your mouth as you stamp kick at the target leg.

After stamp kicking with your skyward leg, bend your knee and place the sole of the boot of your skyward leg on the ground behind your ground contact leg. Make any positional adjustments, breathe in through your nose as you retract and raise your groundward leg. Breathe out through your mouth and adjust your boot toe to point diagonally outwards as you stamp kick with the inner arch of the sole of your boot at the stamp kicking target leg. Retract your leg immediately after stamp kicking.

<u>Instructor checklist: make sure your little soldier...</u>

- Starts the kick lying on their side with their boots facing the bad big person/target.
- Is well within stamp kicking range.
- Tucks both of their legs in close to their body.
- Has their top leg boot flat on ground, bottom boot on ground and against top boot.
- Breathes in through their nose as they pull in and lift their top leg.
- Breathes out through their mouth as they stamp kick the target.
- After kicking with their top leg, bends their upper knee and puts their top boot sole on the ground behind their lower leg.
- Makes adjustments for ground stability and positioning if required.

- Breathes in through their nose as they pull in and raise the bottom leg.
- Breathes out through their nose as they point their bottom leg kicking toes diagonally outwards and stamp kicks the target.
- Uses the arch of their boots when stamp kicking and retracts the leg as soon as they have stamp kicked, taking care not to hyperextend either leg.

CQC SIDE FALLING AND GROUND STAMP KICKING

If you can use your ground falling rocking return action to stamp kick with one or both boots this is a good option.

Always breathe in through your nose as you fall and out through your mouth as you rock back towards the target and stamp kick.

The initial falling action is down and away from your attacker and then as you return rocking back towards your attacker in your side foetal position, stamp kick with both boots using the forward rocking momentum to increase stamp kicking velocity. The kick can be executed with only one leg as well.

If you cannot recover your footing and evade and escape and require continued ground stamp kicks to protect yourself, bend both your knees and keep your legs tucked up close to your body. The sole or side of the sole of your boots will be in contact with the ground for stability and to provide the ability to push away from the bad big person. Position your skyward leg with the knee bent and boot flat on the ground behind your ground closest contact leg. Have the side of your sole of your groundward leg boot in ground contact.

When you stamp kick with one boot, prop by having ground contact with the sole of the other boot for stability and to generate maximum contact impact.

Stamp kick with the arch of your boot's sole and always retract your stamp kicking leg as quickly as you stamp kick with it.

Inhale through your nose as you cock either your ground closest or skyward leg and breathe out through your mouth as you stamp kick with your decided leg.

GROUND MOVEMENT

To move or change your position on the ground, you can use your boots as pictured to ground push and slide away from the bad big person, or you can use your hand to push and slide closer for ground stamp kicking.

If the bad big person tries to move around behind your back you can roll over on your other side, making sure your skyward and groundward legs are bent with your boots in the same position as detailed on the other side and stamp kick.

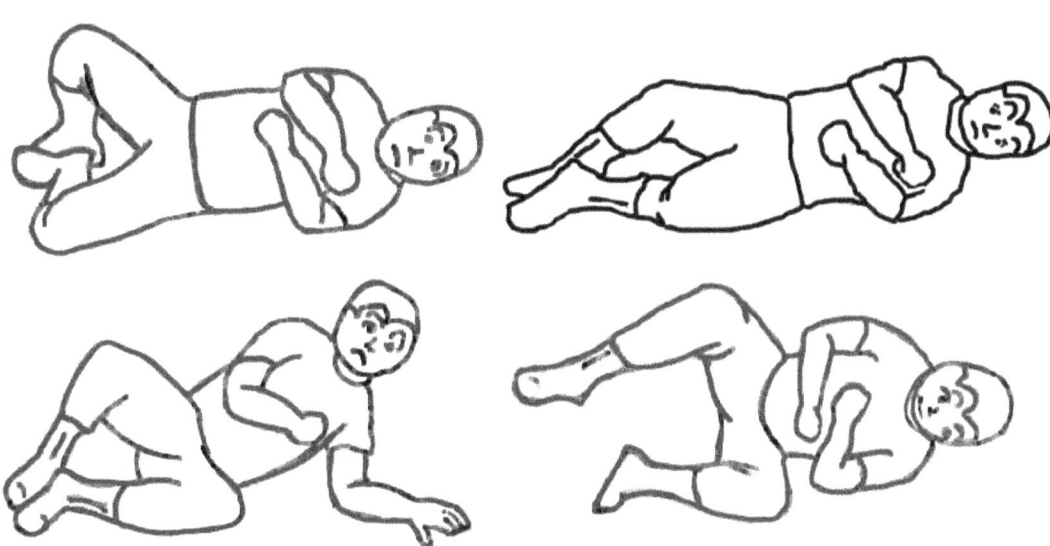

PREVENTING BEING GRABBED AND HELD

To prevent a bad big person from grabbing you from in front, you must inhale through your nose and execute a sudden hard, fast and low squat-crouch. Then slide your boot back to a front stance on your decided direction of evasion. Then exhale out of your mouth, pivot your boots in your decided escape direction, bend forward at the waist away from the bad big person and sprint-start run away. Keep your upper arms and forearms close to your sides and your hands against your tummy until you are far enough away from the bad big person that they cannot grab hold of you.

Once you are out of arms' reach, you can move your arms to your natural running position.

In an emergency such as if the bad big person has gotten too close and you don't have time to slide your boot back and pivot away, after inhaling and squat-crouching you can pivot both your boots diagonally forward so your boots are pointing to the outside of one side of the bad big person in your direction of escape. Then exhale out of your mouth, bend forward at the waist away from the bad big person and sprint-start run diagonally forward and away. Keep your upper arms and forearms tight against your sides and your palms of your hands against your tummy to give the bad big person nothing outstretched to grab hold of.

Suppose a bad big person tries to grab hold of you from the side. To prevent this, inhale and squat-crouch hard and low. Then exhale, pivot both boots diagonally away from the bad big person, bend forward at the waist away from them into a sprint-start position and kick off your sprint-start run escape. As before, keep your upper arms and forearms close to your sides and your hands against your tummy until you are out of arms' reach.

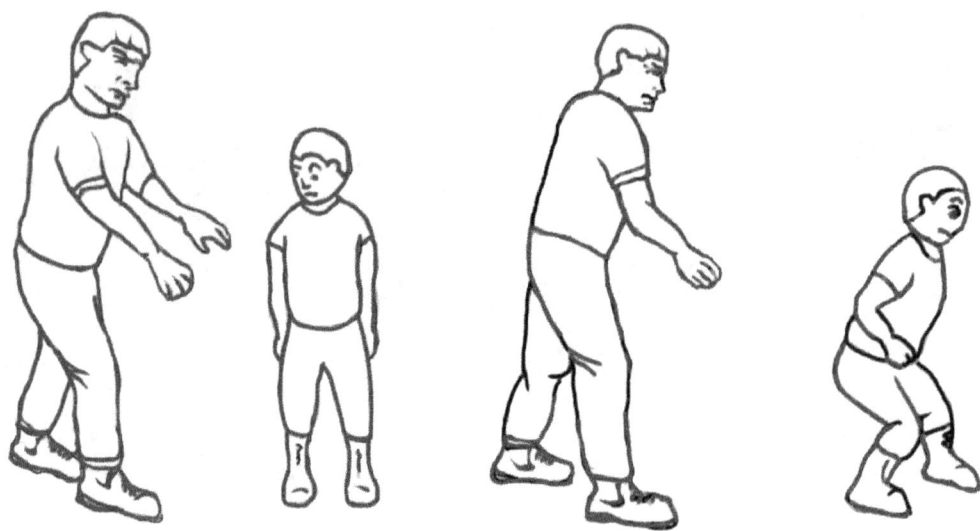

If you detect a bad big person trying to grab hold of you from behind, immediately decide on your direction of escape. Inhale, combined with a hard, fast squat-crouch, exhale, pivot diagonally forward in your decided escape direction and bend forward at the waist away from the bad big person. Keep your arms close to your sides and hands to your tummy and sprint-start run away as fast as you can.

Once there is no danger of being grabbed, you can change your arms to your natural running position.

If the bad big person chases you and is getting close, keep changing direction by zig-zagging to stop them getting hold of you.

<u>Instructor checklist: make sure your little soldier...</u>

- When the bad big person/enemy training per tries to grab them from the front, side or behind, squat-crouches low and hard and breathes in through their nose.

- If the bad big person is in front of or behind your little soldier, slides one boot away from the bad big person to a front stance, unless the bad big person is within emergency range.

- Breathes out as they pivot both boots away in the direction of escape and bends at the waist away from the bad big person. Your little soldier will pivot to the side of the leg that they pulled back if the bad big person is in front or behind them.

- Sprint-start runs away.

- Keeps their upper arms and forearms close to their sides and their hands against their tummy until they are far enough away that they can't be grabbed. Once they are far enough away your little soldier can run naturally.

- Zig-zags while escaping and evading from the bad big person to prevent them getting hold of your little soldier.

RESISTANCE TO COUNTER BEING HELD, PUSHED, PULLED AND LIFTED

You need to make sure that you can stop being lifted from the front, side or behind and resist being pushed or pulled to prevent being abducted.

If a bad big person grabs hold of you by your clothing, around your body only, or around your body and your arms, from the front, then the first thing you need to do is to breathe in and then out as you execute a hard, heavy, fast, low squat-crouch. Simultaneously, as part of your hard-squat crouch, get your head down low and to the side of the bad big person's body. Slide your boot on the same side as your head back into a deep front stance. Make sure the boot that you slide back is the one that is on the same side as your head. For example, if the bad big person has hold of you, and you put your head down by your right shoulder, then you will slide your right boot backwards to a left front stance. If you put your head down by your left shoulder, then you will slide your left boot backwards to a right front stance.

These combined moves are important for making you harder to lift or move.

You must resist being pulled forward towards the bad big person. Pivot your boots diagonally to the same side as your head and the boot that you moved backwards. This puts you into a sprint-start run position. Then resist being pulled forward by hard sprint-start run pushing off diagonally away from the bad big person. Hard boots means hard heavy contact with the ground and a hard heavy continued sprint-start run, kicking off away from them.

If you can break free of their hold on you, sprint-start run away towards help and safety. When you pivot away from the bad big person, be sure to get your head and body over your boot furthermost away from the bad big person and bend your body forward at the waist away from the bad big person. Even if you cannot initially break free, attempting to sprint-run away means that you will be resisting them.

If, however, you are being held and cannot immediately break free from your low pivoted-away position, then slide both of your boots towards the bad big person. Jam your closest boot against their closest leg's boot and stamp kick their lower leg with your closest boot, causing the bad big person to release their hold of you. You may need to stamp kick multiple times to break the bad big person's hold on you. Always adjust your boots to get into range and position. Look and place your stamp kick accurately; do not stamp kick blindly.

When training and practicing, never stamp kick your family army enemy training partner's leg. Instead, simulate the stamp kick slowly and carefully on a soft surface or a soft impact-absorbing target positioned on the ground between you and your acting enemy training partner. When training with an acting enemy training partner, for their safety and yours, stamp kick slowly, correctly and accurately with low-level impact force, to protect yourself and your family army enemy training partner against training injuries.

Never forget to use your self-defence respiration by breathing in with the stamp kick set up and breathing out with the stamp kick execution.

Instructor checklist: make sure your little soldier...

- Breathes in through their nose and out through their mouth as they do a hard, heavy and fast low squat-crouch.

- At the same time, moves their head down low and to the outside of the bad big person's body.

- Slides the boot on the same side as their head back into a deep front stance (e.g. if your little soldier's head is closest to their own right shoulder, they will slide their right leg back and vice versa). This is important for making it harder for the bad big person to lift them.

- Pivots both of their boots to the same side as their head and bends at the waist away from the bad big person. This puts them in the sprint-start run position.

- Resists being pulled forward by hard sprint-start run pushing off the ground diagonally away from the bad big person.

- Resists being pushed backward by stationary resistance from the same sprint start escape position as being pulled forward.

- If they break free, runs to help and safety.

- If your little soldier can't get away from this position, check that they slide their boots towards the bad big person.

- Jams their closest boot against the bad big person's closest target leg boot.

- Adjusts their boots to get into range, position and in balance and looks at the target when stamp kicking.

- Breathes in as they squat-crouch and raise their kicking leg and breathes out as they leg stamp the target leg. This can be done multiple times to make the bad big person let go.

To resist and counter being held, pushed, pulled or lifted from the side, squat-crouch low, hard and fast to prevent being lifted. Pivot away from the bad big person and resist their pushing or pulling action and make any adjustments in range, position and footing to execute a leg stamp kick. Combine this with leg stamping to break their hold on you, then sprint-start run to help and safety.

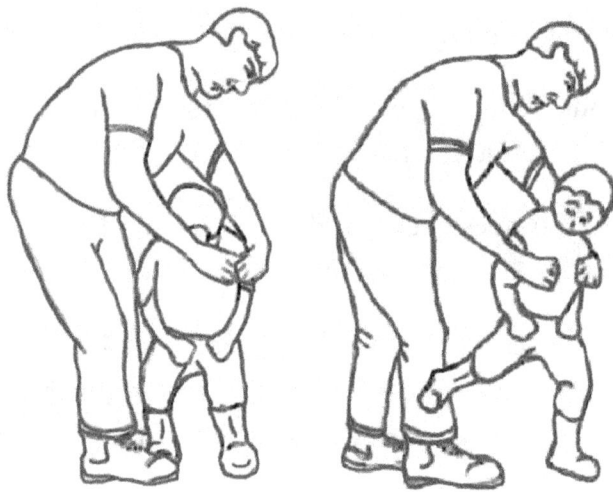

Instructor checklist: make sure your little soldier…

- Breathes in through their nose and out through their mouth as they do a hard, heavy and fast low squat-crouch.

- Pivots away from the bad big person into a diagonal sprint-start run position to resist being pushed, pulled or lifted.

- Moves their closest boot into boot-to-boot contact with the target leg.

- Breathes in as they lift their kicking leg and breathes out as they stamp kick the target closest leg.

- Sprint-start runs to help and safety.

If you are grabbed from your rear flanks and the bad big person is trying to push, pull or lift you. Squat-crouch low, hard and fast and slide one boot forward away from them into a front stance. Pivot slightly diagonally forward to your rear boot side away from the bad big person and resist them. Use stamp kicks, if needed, to help break their hold so that you can sprint-start run to safety.

Knowing how to stand and resist being pushed, pulled or lifted, combined with counter stamp kicks, or army unarmed combat side falling to the ground and ground stamp kicking, makes you a hard target and gives you a better chance of stopping the immediate threat and deciding on the next best means to counter and escape the bad big person.

If the bad big person is trying to lift you off the ground, remember that by fast, hard, heavy and low squat-crouching, you make it much harder for them to lift you. This provides time for you to use the best means of escaping their hold.

Later in this manual you will learn how to escape being held and being held and lifted, but it is most important that you can stop being grabbed or taken away first. To do this you must immediately, with sudden fast, hard and heavy downward shock action, squat-crouch low and follow the previous instructions to counter being grabbed and lifted, pushed or pulled from the front, side or from behind. You may have to squat-crouch more than once to try and prevent being grabbed as well as to make yourself harder to lift or move.

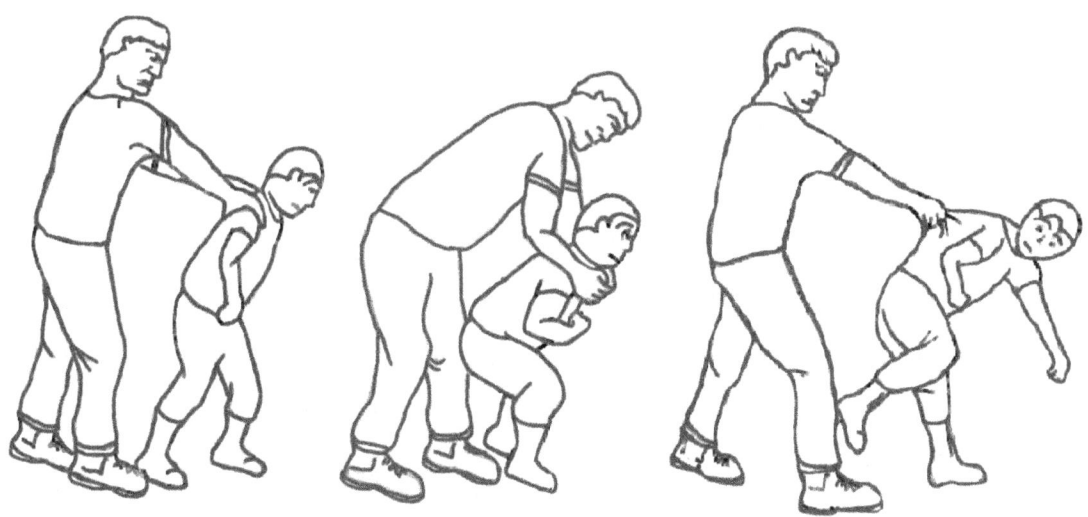

Instructor checklist: make sure your little soldier...

- Breathes in and out while they squat-crouch low, hard and fast, and slides one boot away from the bad big person into a front stance.

- Pivots slightly away from the bad big person to the side of their rearmost boot.

- Adjusts and breathes in as they raise the kicking leg and breathes out as they stamp kick the bad big person's closest target leg.

- Sprint-start runs away to safety.

Being able to stop being lifted and to resist being pushed or pulled is the priority when your little soldier has been seized by a bad big person who wishes to abduct them and/or do them harm.

To escape grabs and holds, your little soldiers will be given counter escape training later in this manual. That training has complete commonality with the preventative and resistance skills discussed here.

It is most important that these primary lifting and moving preventive actions are fully understood and can be executed competently. Start your instruction slowly in parts and then slowly in full. As your little soldier gets more competent and confident, have them increase their speed and their weight-drop momentum until they are hard to lift, get hold of or move.

The family army instructor or training enemy bad big person needs to slowly, with low-level force and intensity, attempt to grab hold of the little soldier around their body from the front and initiate lifting or seize them by the shoulders and initiate pushing or pulling.

Remember, preventative escape measures are the priority. They have commonality with the grabs, holds and abduction counter escape actions that include stamp kicking and side ground falling to prevent or counter abduction, as instructed in this manual.

If the initiated counter action enables evasion and escape, then this is the best option and outcome.

Inhaling and exhaling as they drop their weight can enable slipping downward through the bad big person's hold on them. This, combined with sliding their leg away from the bad big person, can get them closer to the ground, further from the bad big person and break the hold on your little soldier or set up a counter stamp kick and escape.

Safety in training is most important. So, always make sure the training area and the level of enemy bad big person power and force are controlled and safe.

Make sure any stamp kicks or strikes are to training equipment or are simulated in slow motion with low-level contact to the ground or to a positioned impact-absorbent target, so that training partners are not injured.

COUNTER-ABDUCTION RESISTANCE

Little soldiers, we need to make sure that you become a big problem to any bad big person who wants to get hold of you and wants to hurt you.

To do this we need to instruct you on how to make yourself a small, compact, dynamic deadweight. You can do this by inhaling, exhaling and rapid squat-crouching low to the ground, making yourself hard to grab and hard to lift or move if grabbed, like a ship's anchor.

When you inhale, exhale and squat-crouch hard, fast, low and heavy you make yourself a harder target for the bad big person.

Like I told you before, knowing how the bad big person thinks and what they want to do to you can help you to stop them before it happens.

Knowledge, understanding and capability increase your chances of stopping being attacked by preventing or countering an attacker.

You must understand what "abduction" is and be prepared to stop it happening. Abduction is when a bad big person wants to get hold of you and take you with them against your will.

If someone tries to abduct you, the first and best thing to do is to get away before they even touch you or get close to you. If, however, you cannot get away to stop them abducting you, then you might have to stamp-kick and escape or you may need to use an unarmed combat side fall to the ground, commando style.

So, if there are other people nearby, and you cannot get away, then you can fall to the ground commando style, and in your loudest army voice yell out to the people who are nearby and can help you "Help Me! Call The Police! Help Me!"

If you must go to the ground, then always use a side fall, which is the army unarmed combat way to reduce the risk of injury and to keep yourself as safe as possible.

Remember to sidefall from as low to the ground as possible by crouching, squatting, kneeling, pivoting, compressing your body to your thighs and falling on your side, away from the bad big person. Breathe out as you fall and come into contact with the ground in a rocking motion, like a rocking chair.

Practice slowly at first. Then, as you get more confident and competent you can fall faster.

After falling and ground stamp kicking, if you can recover your footing to a sprint-start evasion and escape position then do so and sprint-run off for safety and to get help.

To get clear of the bad big person, you can barrel roll (or "gator roll" as it is also known) to the side away from the bad big person, then get up and sprint run away. After you barrel roll several times to the side away from the bad big person, make sure your boots are facing them in case you need to ground counter stamp kick before rolling over, getting up and sprint running away.

To barrel roll away, grasp the back of your head and neck with the palms of your hands in a cover guard to make barrel rolling faster, safer and easier.

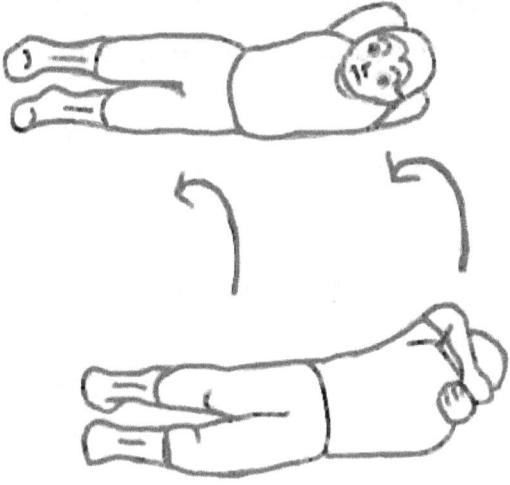

Let me repeat, as soon as it is safe to do so, if help is available, call for help, "Help Me! Call The Police! Help Me"

COUNTER-ABDUCTION RESISTANCE AND GROUND SIDE FALLING FROM FRONT ON

Little soldier, stand in front of the stamp kick impact cushion or half buried tyre with the instructor in front of you holding onto both your wrists and simulating pulling you towards them.

You must squat-crouch, pivot away from the instructor and resist with your boots by pushing hard into the ground and pushing away from the instructor. If you are pulled toward the instructor, however, then you must slide your boots while resisting, and when you are in contact range, stamp kick the target from the squat-crouch position. Immediately after the pivoted squat-crouch, stamp kick and rapidly sprint run away to safety.

Once you can effectively do this then after the stamp kick, side fall to the ground away from their instructor. Then, stamp kick the target from the ground. This is practice to ensure that you know how to continue if your initial standing stamp kick fails, or if you end up on the ground.

Immediately after side falling, use the boot of the leg closest to the sky, or use both boots, to stamp kick low and hard at the impact target to get free. Kick multiple times if required, then prop with the skyward leg behind the groundward leg and push hard into the ground away from the stamp kicking impact target. With the boot of the leg closest to the ground, stamp kick with the arch of the sole of the boot at the stamp kicking target. Barrel roll away several times making sure your boots are facing the bad big person. Then recover your footing and sprint-start escape.

Family army instructor, you should straddle the half-buried car tyre, impact target or a ground-positioned cushion impact target. Make sure that your feet and legs are well clear of the little soldier's stamp kick and brief the little soldier that they must stamp kick accurately on the target. Having a bullseye or crosshairs on your impact target will improve accuracy and increase safety.

Practice this with the instructor enemy person holding one of the little soldier's wrists with either one hand or both hands. Practice also with the instructor enemy person holding both of the little soldier's wrists.

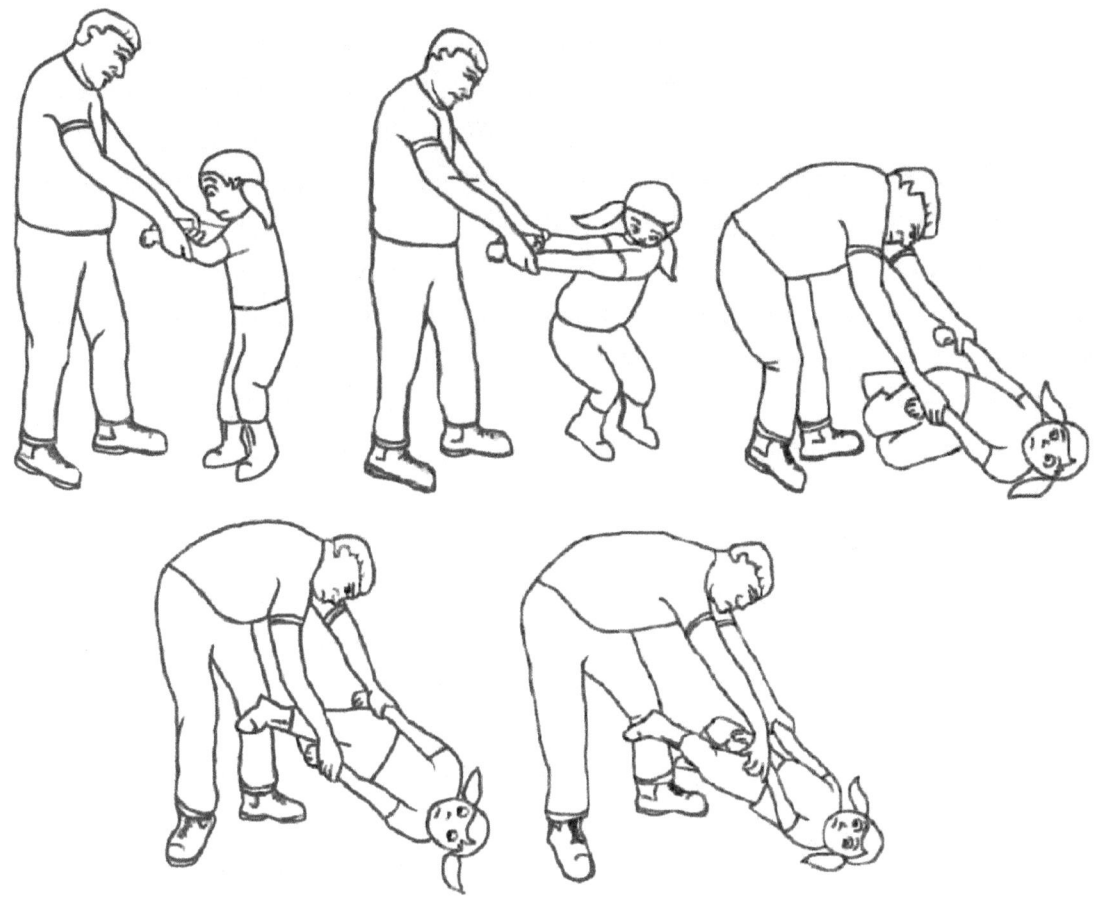

COUNTER-ABDUCTION RESISTANCE AND GROUND SIDE FALLING FROM SIDE ON

Little soldier, when seized and secured from the side, you should squat-crouch, pivot away and resist by pushing hard into the ground away from your instructor enemy training per. Then side fall away from your instructor. Be aware that when your instructor is pulling, you may slide along the ground towards them. Execute the same stamp kicks as you did for the front-on counter abduction resistance.

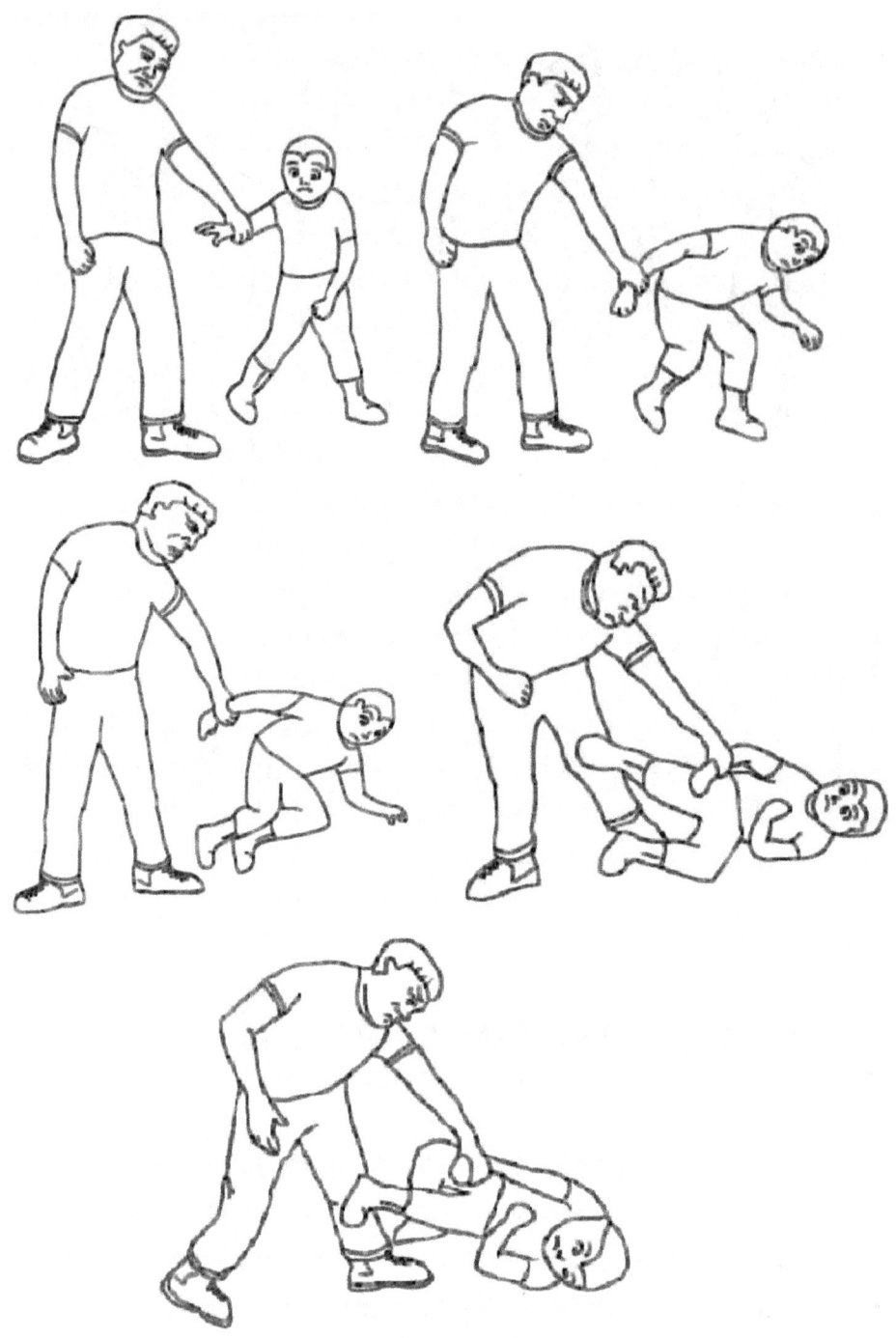

If you are grabbed by the hair from the side, seize and secure the bad big person's wrist or wrists and hold their hand or hands down against your head to reduce the pain of your hair being pulled. Employ the same squat-crouch pivot away stamp kicking and/or ground stamp kicking that you did when your wrist or wrists were being seized.

If you are grabbed by the hair from the front or the rear, then turn side on, pivot, and execute the same counter skills.

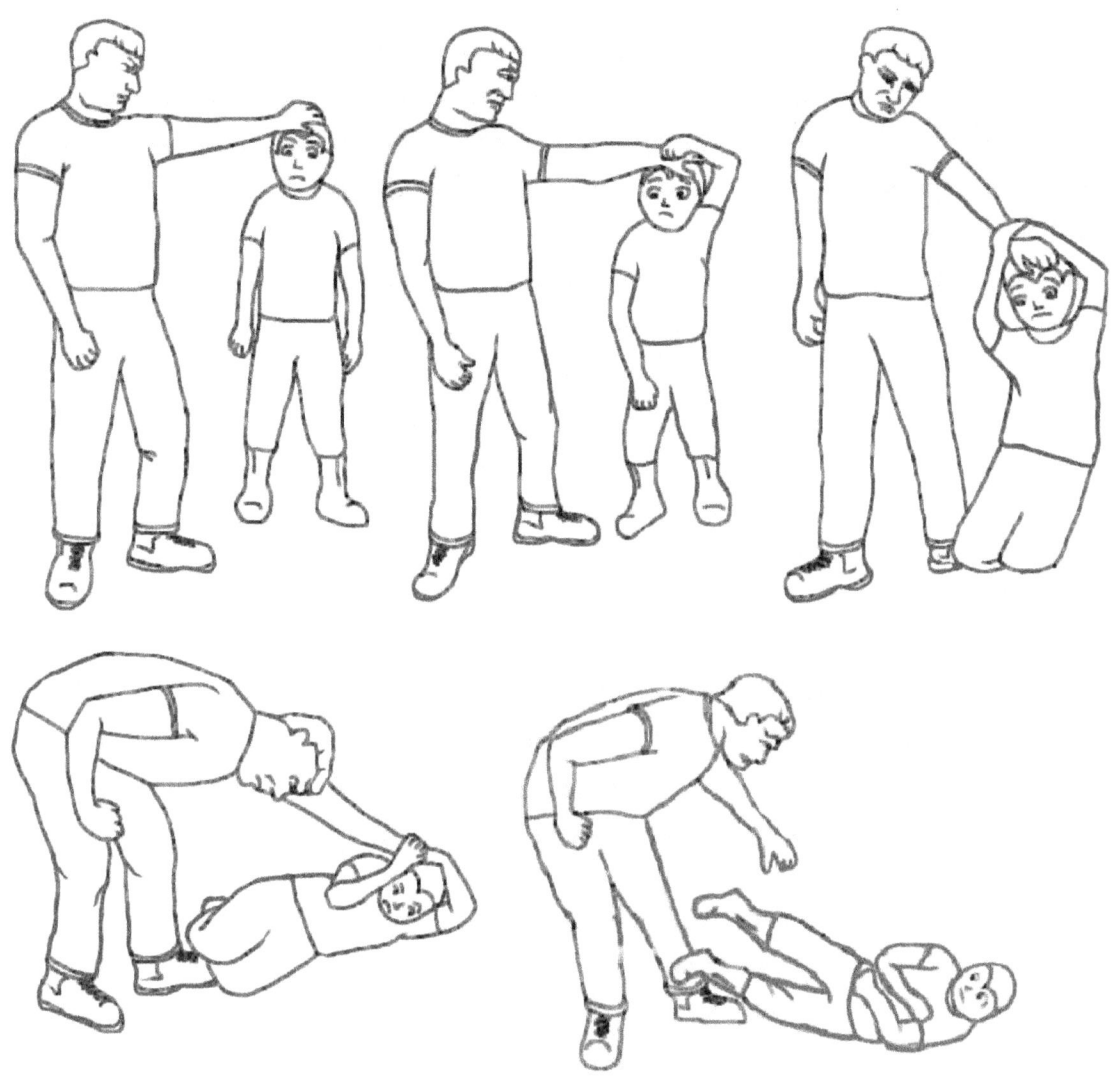

COUNTER-ABDUCTION RESISTANCE AND GROUND SIDE FALLING FROM YOUR REAR FLANKS

Little soldier, if you are grabbed by the shoulders or clothes from behind, you will squat-crouch and slide your non-stamp kicking boot forward away from the enemy per. Resist by pushing hard into the ground away from the enemy per. Now pivot, getting into a stamp-kick execution position, and stamp kick the impact target.

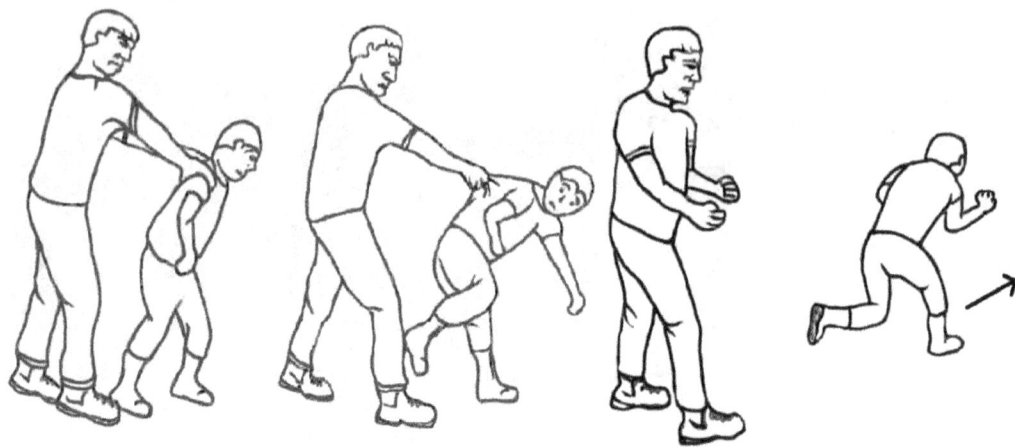

If it is not possible to stamp kick, because of being dragged and being off balance, then squat-crouch low and hard, pivot away from the training enemy per and side fall to the ground from as low to the ground as possible, stamp kick and escape. If you cannot immediately escape make sure that you adjust your footing to get your boots in close to the training enemy per's boots, and stamp kick the training target in the same way as with frontal and side counter-abduction resistance ground side falling and ground stamp kicking.

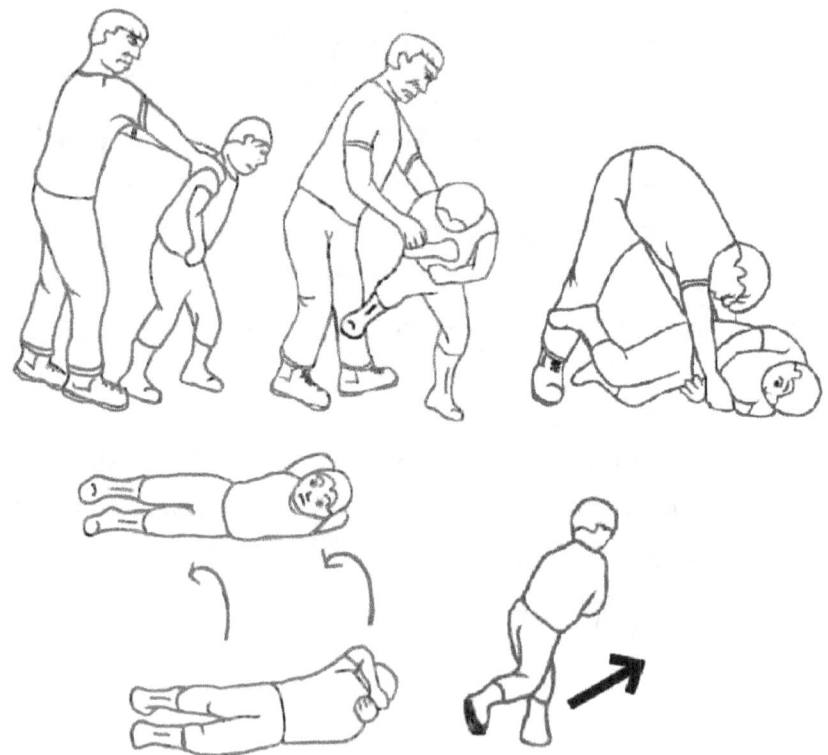

If both of your wrists are seized from behind, then squat-crouch and employ running away resistance and a stamp kick if possible. If you cannot stamp kick, then from a squat crouch you should side fall, secure the palm of your hand furthest away from the enemy per on your bottom or grab hold of your trouser belt or waistband. This will reduce the likelihood of a painful elbow-to-ground contact. On falling, your arm closest to the ground will be down your side and behind your back. Set up, make adjustments and execute ground stamp kicks to break the bad big person's hold on you and sprint run escape, or barrel roll away and then recover your footing and sprint run away.

Instructor, seize one wrist and one shoulder or upper arm of your little soldier from behind. The little soldier will be standing with their back to you. The stamp kicking target will be half buried in the ground or will be free standing secured between your legs. You can be either standing and straddling the impact target or seated on the target straddling it. Now try it again with both of your little soldier's wrists seized from their flanks.

Instructor checklist: make sure your little soldier...

- Squat crouches when seized by the bad big person/enemy training per, pivots and resists by pushing into the ground with their boots away from the bad big person.

- If seized by the hair, locks their hands down against the bad big person's hands to minimise the pain of having their hair pulled.

- If the furthest away hand from the bad big person is free, locks this hand against their bottom or belt to prevent painful elbow contact with the ground.

- Makes range, breathes in and breathes out as they stamp kick the closest target leg if needed to weaken the bad big person's grip so they can evade and escape or side fall and use ground counter-abduction stamp kicks.

- Squat crouches as low to the ground as they can and army side falls to the ground, away from the bad big person.

- Spins on their side if needed to bring their boots closest to the bad big person.

- Breathes in, pulls back the upper leg and breathes out as they stamp kick the closest target leg.

- Moves the upper skyward leg in behind the lower groundward leg, placing the skyward boot on the ground for stability.

- Breathes in and pulls back the lower groundward leg then breathes out and oblique leg stamps the closest leg.

- Keeps kicking until they can break free and escape by barrel rolling away and using sprint-start run evasion and escape.

VEHICLE/HOUSE/BUILDING ABDUCTION PREVENTION

If a bad big person lifts you off the ground from behind and is carrying you towards a car, house, building or away from where there are people to help you, then try to make them let go of you by using swinging leg raises, lifting knee raises and smashing heels stamp kicks at their shins.

If this makes the bad big person put you down or let go of you, then squat-crouch and pivot in the direction you will escape to, and sprint-start run away to safety, or pivot, stamp kick and escape run away.

If you are still being held and can get the soles of your boots and palms of your hands on the ground, then you can monkey walk away and stamp kick at the bad big person's shins.

From low to the ground or kneeling, you can pivot to the side you want to fall on and side fall away from the bad big person and ground stamp kick to make them let go. If they let go, you can sprint-start run away or barrel roll to one side or the other and sprint-start run away.

From the side fall position, you can roll onto your belly and commando crawl and ground stamp kick to make them let go, so that you can get away.

Lying flat on your belly you can look back and push with the arches of the soles of your boots against the bad big person's lower legs, making it hard for them to lift or move you and you can then stamp kick their lower legs by carefully looking on the side you will stamp kick before you stamp kick.

Remember to always use controlled close combat breathing, and stamp kick as many times as it takes to make them let go of you, so that you can get away.

If the bad big person is holding you from behind with your boots off the ground and they are trying to put you in a car or building, you can stamp push kick against the closed car door or closed building door to stop them opening it.

Stamp push kick on the door or door frame close to the opening to stop them opening it.

If the bad big person is opening the door with one hand and holding you off the ground with the other, then you can stamp kick their fingers and thumbs and the car door to make them let go of you.

Always try to stamp push kick on or near the door opening. This could be at the top, bottom, middle or side of the door, depending upon where and how high or low you are being held off the ground.

If your stamp kicking resistance against the door pushes you and the bad big person back from the door, and if you can get the soles of your boots on the ground in a very low-to-the-ground seated position, then push into the ground with the soles of your boots to resist being moved back towards the car or building.

If you are being pushed to a car or building and you are in a low sitting position, pivot, turn on your side and side fall.

If the bad big person still has hold of you, resist by pushing the soles of your boots into the ground. Use the sole of one boot to resist and the other to stamp push kick against the door. Keep stamp push kicking against the bottom of the door or sill. As soon as you get free sprint-start run escape.

Stamp kick resist against the bottom of the door or the door sill or the car's tyre if it is in range. As soon as you can get free, sprint-start run escape.

Vehicle abduction prevention also applies to your little soldier being forcefully taken to a building or into any out-of-public-sight concealed area.

Importantly, your little soldier needs to be the hardest target possible as soon as they identify the bad big person trying to seize them. Prevention and escape is always the best option for them. As soon as they identify the bad big person making an approach or grab at them, they need to squat-crouch, pivot away from the bad big person in the direction of their escape and sprint-start run away to safety, effectively preventing the bad big person getting hold of them.

Vehicles, buildings or concealed areas abduction prevention uses similar practices and principles to the previous lifting or moving counter skills. These skills are, however, combined with the addition of using the soles of the boots and legs to push off or achieve movement resistance by stamping pushing against the vehicle, building, tree, structures, posts or poles and locking the legs in position.

This stamp kicking resistance action is done by retracting both legs with knees bent up towards the body and then thrusting them out, contacting the solid structure with the soles of the boots. This action is different to stamp kicking a bad pig person's leg where you are trying to injure them, because the car building or tree is much bigger and stronger. You do not want to injure your foot or leg so the stamp kick action must be a hard pushing action.

Your little soldiers' stamp and push-off resistance on vehicles with the door closed should be against the closed door. Push stamp kick resistance by keeping their legs and boots locked tight together will reduce leg injuries and increase single direct point impact.

The best part of the door for them to aim their boots at is on the door close to the door jamb opening.

If the bad big person is attempting to open the car door while holding your little soldier, they can target the door-opening hand with one boot and the door jamb with the other.

If your little soldier has managed to get down to a close-to-the-ground or ground-seated position, with their boot soles pushing hard into the ground away from the vehicle, they should pivot to side on and stamp push kick resist with one boot at the bottom of the vehicle door. If the door is open, they should stamp push kick at the door pillar or door sill below the door while pushing away and resisting with the other boot.

The same practice applies to buildings, trees, posts, poles or any structures to prevent being taken.

If your little soldier's position is on the ground close to the vehicle's wheel, they can stamp push kick resist against the car tyre or wheel.

The important thing is for your little soldier to target solid immovable parts of the vehicle, building or structure to prevent the door being opened, or to prevent being forced into the vehicle or building if the door is already open.

Doorsteps, door frames, walls, car sills, door pillars and tree trunks are all best options for push stamp kicking abduction resistance.

If your little soldier is being held off the ground and the bad big person is trying to take them away or put them inside a vehicle or building, the stamp push kicking resistance may have to be directed at the door pillar or immediately above the opened door on the door frame.

This may require turning and twisting of the torso and split-boot resistance stamp push kicking, where, for example, one boot sole may be on the top door frame and the other on the door pillar.

Ideally, for safety and generating the most effective impact resistance, having both legs and boots together is best for preventative resistance force generation.

For targeting the bad big person's fingers or thumbs a single boot contact impact will work well.

It is important to select the best position to stamp push kick resist. The objective is to enable a release and escape or get on the ground outside the door and continue to push off low and strong away from the vehicle or building entry point.

If your little soldier ends up between a door and the inside of a vehicle it is important that they employ the same stamp push kicking resistance as quickly as possible against the inner door, inner edge of the door pillar, door jamb, sill, seat, dashboard, steering wheel or any other robust surface.

I recommend that they do not wrap their arms around a vehicle open window frame or a door pillar or steering wheels as the door being jammed against your little soldier will cause immense pain. The resulting pain and probable injury would most likely cause them to let go of their hold and as such they would end up in the vehicle or in the building.

The primary objectives are to prevent abduction and to get away. Using their longest strongest limbs (that is, their legs) and the soles of their boots is consistent with prevention as well as with counter actions and with getting away. If they are at risk of a door jamming injury, stamp push kicking the inside of the door is best.

Any time your little soldier can target the bad big person's fingers and thumbs as part of their resistance by stamp kicking, this should be undertaken as this can cause immediate grip release and can produce painful incapacitation injuries.

COUNTERING A REAR FLANK BODY HOLD

If a bad big person tries to pick you up from behind around your tummy in one move, you should quickly squat-crouch and drop your body forward, downward and away from the bad big person. Thrust your legs back between their legs, kicking the inside of the bad big person's lower legs with the heels of your boots. Commando side fall to the ground and ground stamp kick. To escape, you can roll over onto your tummy and quickly sprint-start run away or commando crawl away, recover your footing and sprint off. From your tummy, in a commando crawl position, you can turn to one side, look back under your armpit and stamp at the bad big person's legs. Dropping groundward fast and hard significantly increases your weight for a fraction of a second and increases your chances of breaking the bad big person's hold on you.

If you are grabbed in a bear hug from behind, and your arms are pinned to your body, then after hard squat-crouching forward, downward and away from the bad big person, thrust stamp kick back at their inner lower legs, bend and free your arms up, over and out of the bad big persons' hold, then employ the same actions as with a rear body hold if your arms are free.

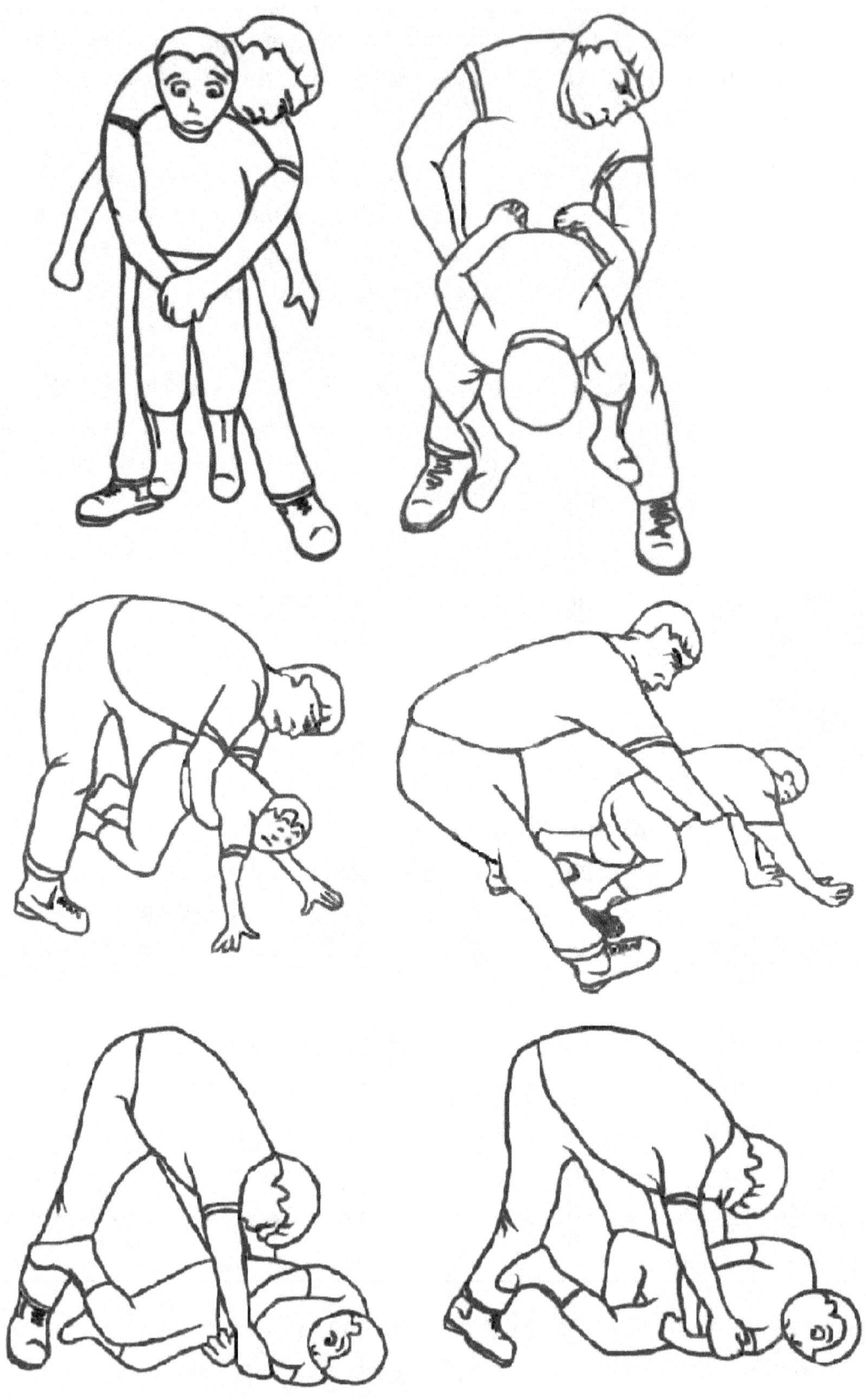

By dropping hard and fast you are doing the unexpected and increasing your chances of stopping the attack.

If they keep hold of you when your feet are on the ground or they hold you slightly off the ground, resist by trying to sprint away. If your boots cannot touch the ground, then wiggle, squiggle and wriggle violently from side to side and up and down. Try to find any gap in the bad big person's hold on you through which you can escape or get down to the ground.

Now try to commando crawl or monkey walk away from the bad big person as Hard and fast as you can.

Look to one side and stamp kick back if you can't immediately get away. All the time you should be raising the alarm by yelling "Help Me! Get The Police, Help Me!'.

Instructor checklist: make sure your little soldier...

- Quickly squat-crouches, drops their body forward, downward and away from the bad big person.

- Thrusts their legs back between the bad big person's legs, kicking the inside of the bad big person's lower legs with the heels of their boots.

- Commando side falls to the ground and ground stamp kicks.

- Rolls onto their tummy and quickly sprint start runs away.

- Or from the commando crawl position, looks back under their arm and stamp kicks the bad big person's lower leg.

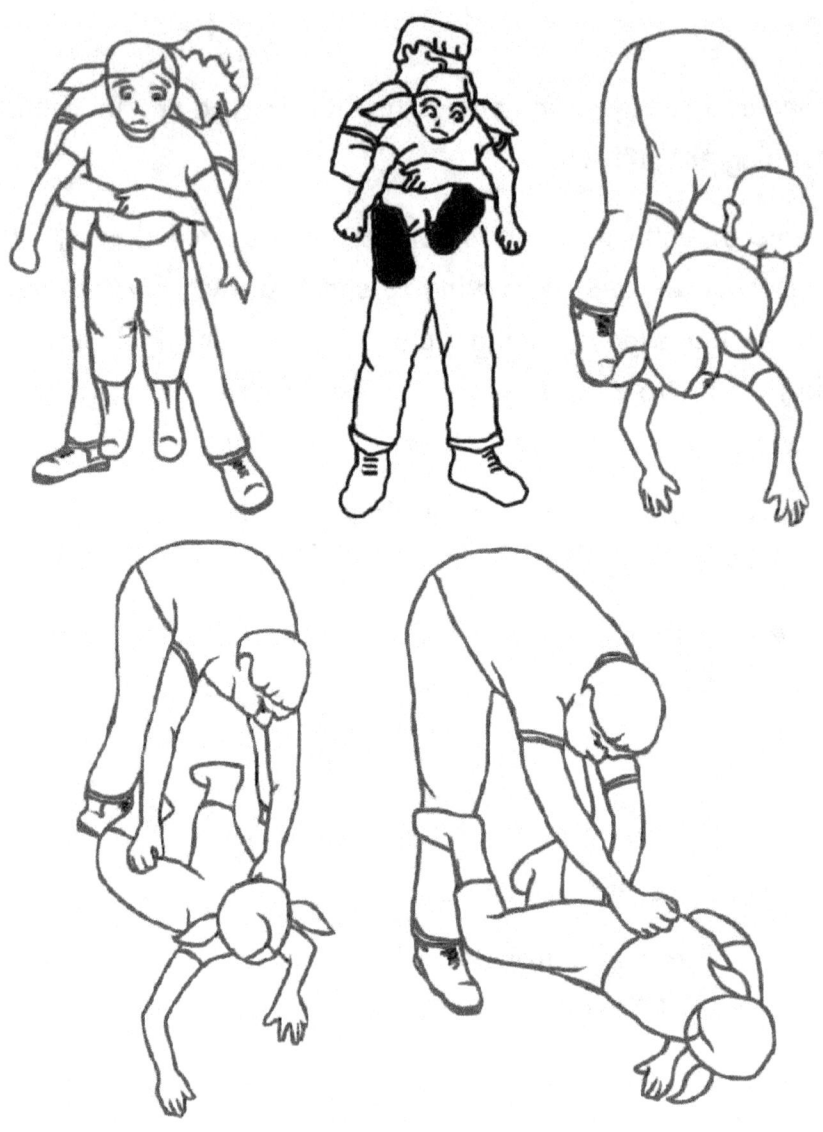

If a bad big person picks you up from behind, holding you high up around your chest from behind so that you cannot drop forward at the waist to a commando crawling position on the ground, then you need to do the following.

Raise both your legs straight up and out in front of you and then swing them back and downward, smashing the heels of your boots into the bad big person's inner lower legs.

If they are still holding you upright, then repeat the raising of your legs and smashing the heels of your boots back at their inner lower legs until their hold on you is weakened. Then you can employ the next part of the escape. Remember to breathe in with every leg lift and out with every backward swinging heels kicking action.

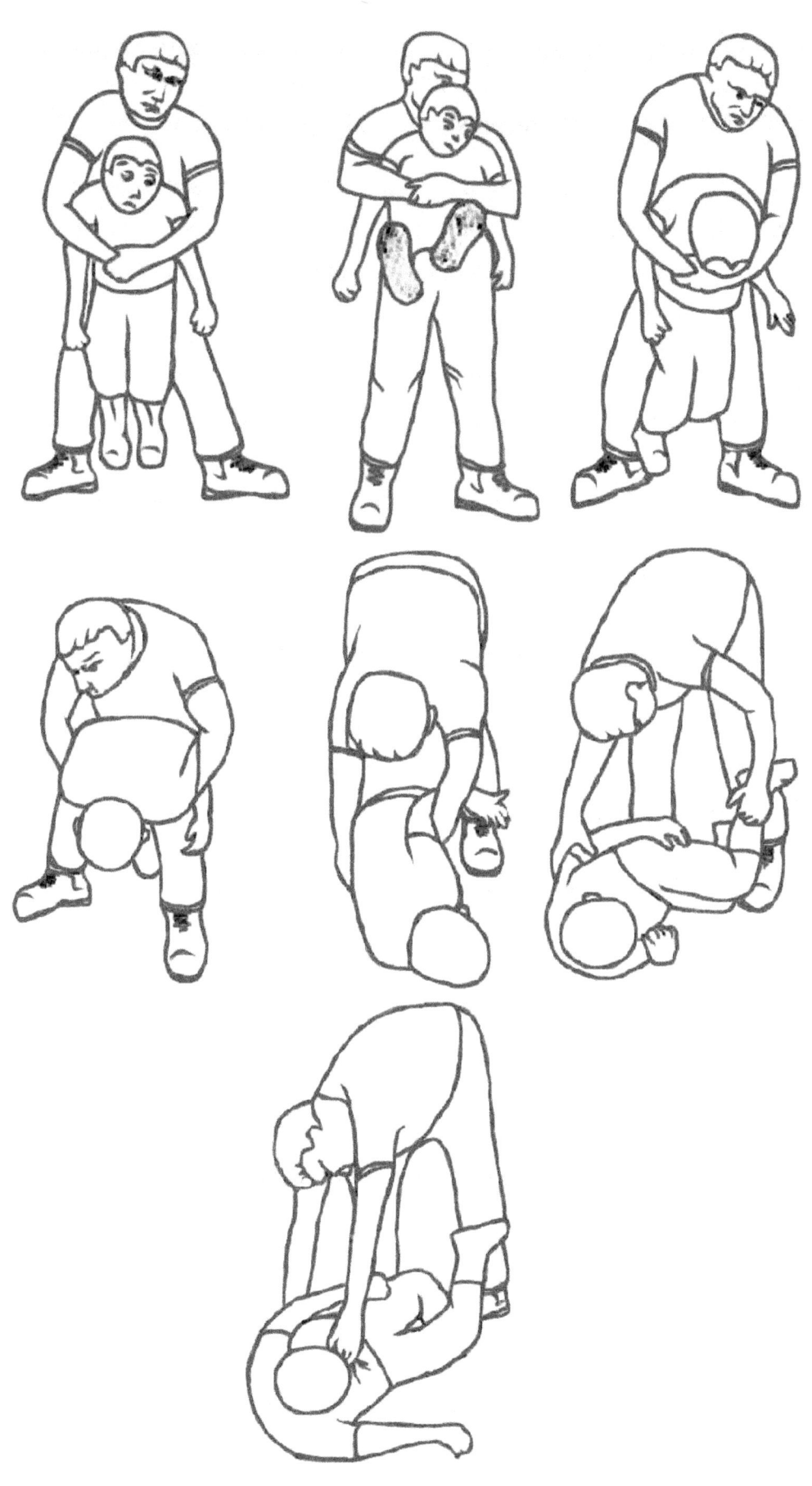

If you can break the bad big person's hold and get into a ready-set-go squat-crouch sprint run start position, the next part of the escape is to sprint away to safety and raise the alarm, thereby getting help.

Remember you can wriggle, wiggle and squiggle down groundward until your boots touch the ground and then shimmy out of the hold on you to a sprint-start ready-set-go position and run away. Keep low to the ground and compact, making it harder for the bad big person to get hold of you again.

If you cannot sprint away, the next part of the escape action is to drop forward by side falling to the ground, away from the bad big person. Then get as low as a snake's belly to the ground, in a commando crawl position. Then commando crawl or barrel roll away. If you still cannot get away, then turn to one side and stamp kick or prop resist, and stamp kick back at your attacker's lower legs until you can escape.

Remember to yell for help if there is help close by "Help Me! Get the Police! Help me!"

<u>Instructor checklist: make sure your little soldier...</u>

- Raises both of their legs straight out in front of them then swings them back and downwards, smashing the heels of their boots into the bad big person's lower legs. Your little soldier can repeat this as many times as needed to weaken the bad big person's grip.

- Breathes in when lifting their legs and breathes out when kicking with their heels.

- If they can break away, gets into a sprint-start run position, then sprints away to safety and help.

- If they can't get away, check they turn to one side and stamp kick at the bad big person's lower leg joints and sprint start run escape.

- If they still can't sprint away, check your little soldier drops forward by side falling to the ground away from the bad big person and commando crawls or barrel rolls away.

COUNTERING A BODY HOLD FROM THE FRONT

If a bad big person picks you up from the front with their arms around your arms so that your arms are pinned to your body, you need to employ the following escape.

Position your hands on the bad big person's back or side for safety. Wrap one of your legs around the outside of the bad big person's directly opposite leg. Remember to breathe, inhale and exhale, then knee them in the groin with your other leg, then knee them again and again, exhaling with every knee to the groin. Keep doing that until their hold weakens.

When their hold on you weakens, raise one shoulder and lower the other, squiggling, wriggling and wiggling from side to side and up and down as you shimmy down toward the ground to escape their hold on you. You can use your hands around the bad big person's sides or the back of their body to aid in shimmying down like a fireman sliding down a fireman's pole. Steadying yourself when you slide down helps to prevent you falling backwards to the ground and landing on the back of your head, neck and spine.

When you are on the ground, sprint-run away. If this is not possible, then commando crawl, monkey walk or barrel roll away. When you are out of reach and far enough away from the bad big person, get up and sprint-start run to escape to safety.

When the bad big person releases their hold on you, place one or both palms around their back or sides so as to steady yourself when you slide down the bad big person's body. Slide down or wiggle, squiggle and slide down, pivot and turn in your escape direction and sprint start run away.

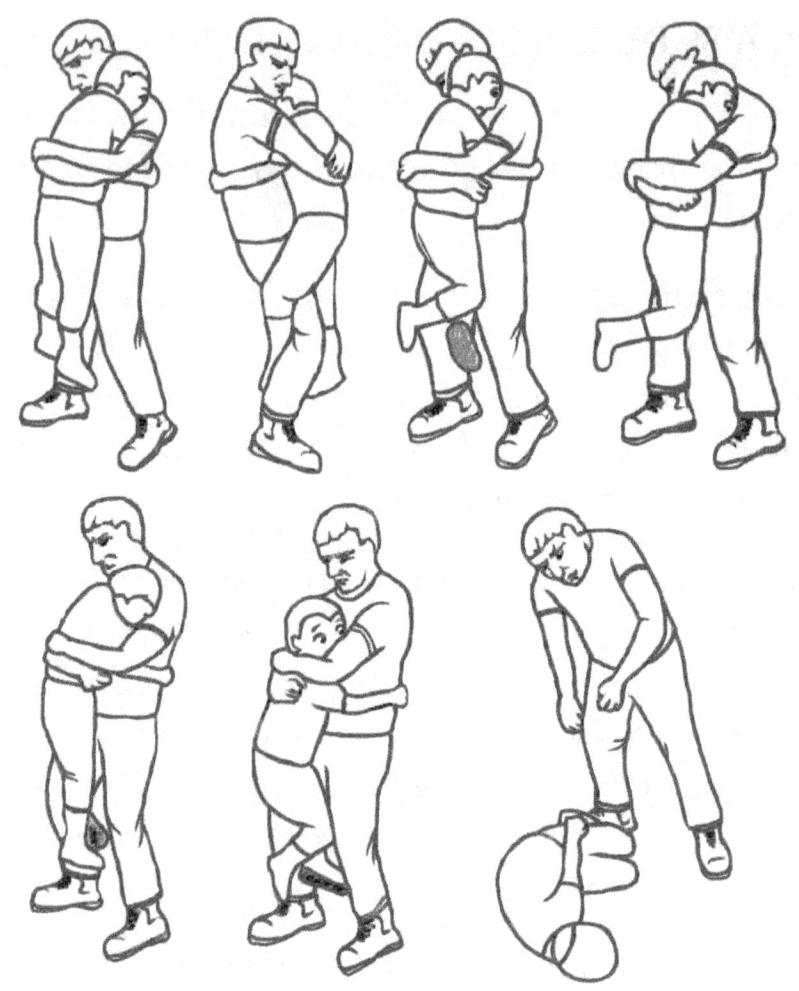

If you are picked up in a belly-to-belly body hold with your arms or one arm free, use the same initial skills as if your arms were pinned. Use your arms and hands or one arm and hand to prevent being thrown or falling backwards by clinging to the bad big person's back or side. Wrap one leg around the bad big person's leg while kneeing to the groin. Remember to breathe in and exhale when kneeing them. One arm/hand will be around the bad big person's side or back, while the other can be used to eye spike. To eye spike form a fist with the thumb on top of the side of the index finger and hard pressed against it and the tip of the thumb extended as far forward of it as possible. From as close as possible poke the eye with the tip of the thumb. Inhale, exhale and knee strike, then inhale, exhale and knee strike, then inhale, exhale and knee strike, and with every knee strike you should follow up with a thumb-spike in the eye.

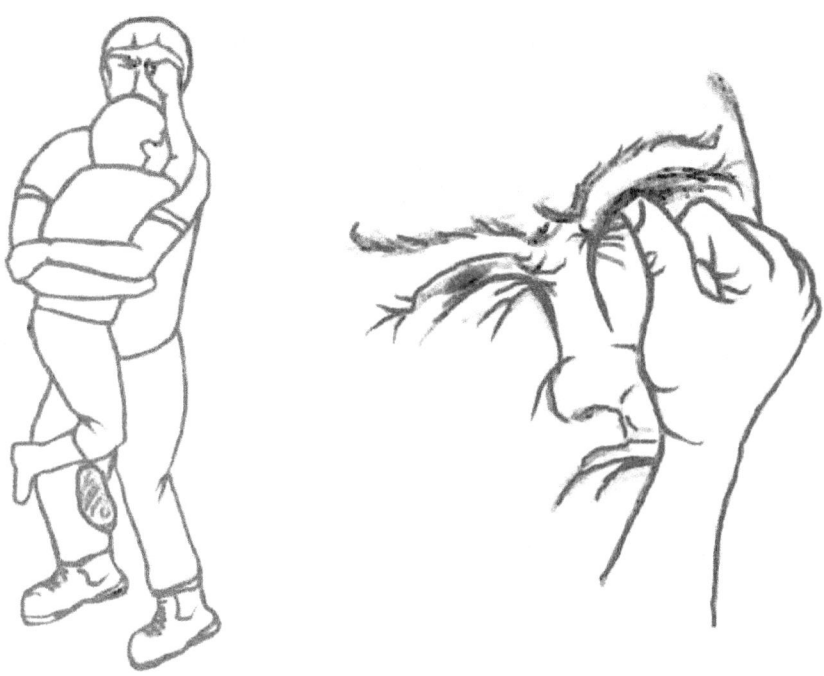

Keep your body long and streamlined like an eel wriggling and slithering downward to escape the bad big person's hold on you.

The groundward action can take you to different positions. For example, you could end up in a squat-crouched sprint-start evasion and escape position, where you can turn away from the bad big person, facing in the direction you can escape by sprinting off. When sprinting off, you may go in a straight-line or, if pursued by the bad big person, you can zig-zag, changing your direction.

If you cannot break their hold on you but can get your boot soles on the ground, you can squat-crouch and ground push resist, pivot and stamp kick to break their hold on you and sprint run escape to safety.

Alternatively, if you cannot escape their grasp or prevent continued abduction attempts, then you might end up going to the ground and commando crawling, monkey walking or barrel rolling to get far enough away to recover your footing and sprint-start run away to safety. If you go to the ground and cannot get away, ground stamp kicks at the bad big person's lower legs can be employed and the alarm can be raised by yelling "Help Me! Get The Police! Help Me!"

Instructor checklist: make sure your little soldier...

- Wraps one of their legs around the outside of the bad big person's opposite leg.

- Breathes in through their nose and out through their mouth.

- Knees the bad big person in the groin repeatedly until their hold weakens.

- If their arms are free, they should thumb spike the bad big person's eye each time they knee them in the groin.

- When their hold weakens, raises one shoulder and lowers the other repeatedly to wriggle and squiggle from side to side and up and down as they shimmy downwards towards the ground to escape the hold.

- Can use their hands around the bad big person's sides or back to help slide down like a fireman sliding down a fireman's pole. This prevents them falling backwards onto their head or neck.

- Once they hit the ground, sprint-start runs away.

- If they can't immediately sprint-start run away, squat-crouches, resists, pivots and stamp kicks from a squat-crouch position and sprint run escapes. Failing this they can side fall and commando crawl, monkey walk or barrel roll away then get up and sprint-start run to safety.

ABDUCTION PREVENTION FROM THE SIDE USING BOOTS AND MITTS

If a bad big person tries to abduct you using a bear hug or another body hold and if you can "hit the deck" (that means get down on the ground on your belly) the boots and mitts method of seizing and securing both the bad big person's lower legs will make it very hard for them to move you.

The boots and mitts position is when your arms are wrapped around one leg and your legs are wrapped around the other leg with your ankles crossed. It stops or makes it hard for a bad big person to move you, and it puts you in a position where you can stamp kick the bad big person's lower leg, regain your footing and escape-runaway to safety.

Follow the steps below slowly, carefully and safely to learn this way to stop a bad big person from abducting you.

As soon as you are seized around the body, or around the body and arms, squat-crouch and thrust your legs backward as hard and fast as you can, getting down on the ground as low as a snake's belly.

You need to be careful not to hurt yourself during this fast, hard-falling action.

To reduce the risk of injury, squat-crouch as low as you can, keeping your knees off the ground surface and then thrust your legs backwards out straight to a lying flat on the ground position, with one leg on each side of the bad big person's leg.

The most important thing is that you safely, but hard and fast, get down flat on the ground. This can be done by side falling and then rolling over on your tummy or by direct squat-thrusts that allow you to fall flat on your tummy. If you are held belly to belly you might be able to wiggle and squiggle and slide down to the ground.

Your head can be positioned in front of the bad big person's lower legs or behind their lower legs. If your head is behind their lower legs, it will be more difficult for them to strike you with their hands.

As soon as you can see their closest leg, secure the leg with both arms wrapped around the leg by seizing as low down on the leg as possible; tightly hug and hold the leg.

If your hold on the leg is above the knee or is in the back of the knee joint, you can slide your hands/arms down the lower leg before or after you wrap your legs around the bad big person's other leg.

After securing the bad big person's leg with your arms, look back and wrap your legs around their other leg, crossing your ankles.

This position will make it very hard for the bad big person to move you and it will stop or slow down an abduction attempt.

You can adjust your position, from on your side to on your belly or from on your belly to on your side, to best get hold of and keep hold of the bad big person's legs.

Once you have stopped them moving you, you can use stamp kicking to make them let go of you and they may fall down. Then you can get back to your feet and sprint-run away to safety.

You can stamp kick with the sole of one or both boots or you can use the boot closest to the ground to hook around the outside of the bad big person's ankle, combined with stamp kicking below their knee joint with your boot closest to the sky. Immediately after they let go of you, regain your footing and sprint run evade and escape.

Ground stamp kicking below the bad big person's knee joint should cause them to fall away from you. If the kick makes them bend and fall forward you need to barrel roll away so they don't fall on you, then recover your footing and sprint-run to safety.

<u>Instructor checklist: make sure your little soldier…</u>

- Immediately after being grabbed around the body or body and arms squat crouches and thrusts their legs backwards as hard and fast as they can. Check they squat crouch as low as they can before thrusting the legs backwards on each side of the bad big person's leg if possible and keep their knees off of the ground to prevent ground contact injury.

- If your little soldier is held belly to belly, they may need to wiggle and squiggle and slide down the bad big person to get to the ground. They may do this after kneeing and eye spiking as previous if they can't get away.

- If they have gone to the ground, as soon as they see the closest leg, check your little soldier grabs it with both arms, wrapping them around the leg as low down as possible. Check they tightly hug the leg.

- Once they are on the ground, their head can be in front or behind the bad big person's legs, however if their head is behind their attacker's legs it makes it harder for the bad big person to strike your little soldier.

- Looks back and wraps their legs around the bad big person's other leg by crossing their ankles. This makes it very hard for the bad big person to move your little soldier and will stop or slow down an abduction attempt.

- If needed, they can adjust their position from side on to belly facing downwards to keep hold of the bad big person's legs.

- When they have stopped the bad big person from moving them, they can use stamp kicks to make them let go, recover their footing and sprint-start run away to safety. Your little soldier can stamp kick with one or both boots or use their bottom boot to hook around the bad big person's ankle and stamp kick with the top boot.

COUNTERING BEING ABDUCTED BY YOUR ANKLES

If a bad big person gets hold of one or both of your ankles when you are lying on the ground, or after you have been pushed or fallen to the ground, then you need to barrel roll multiple times to break their grip on your ankles. You may need to barrel roll several times to one side and if that does not break their hold on you then reverse direction and barrel roll several times to the other side.

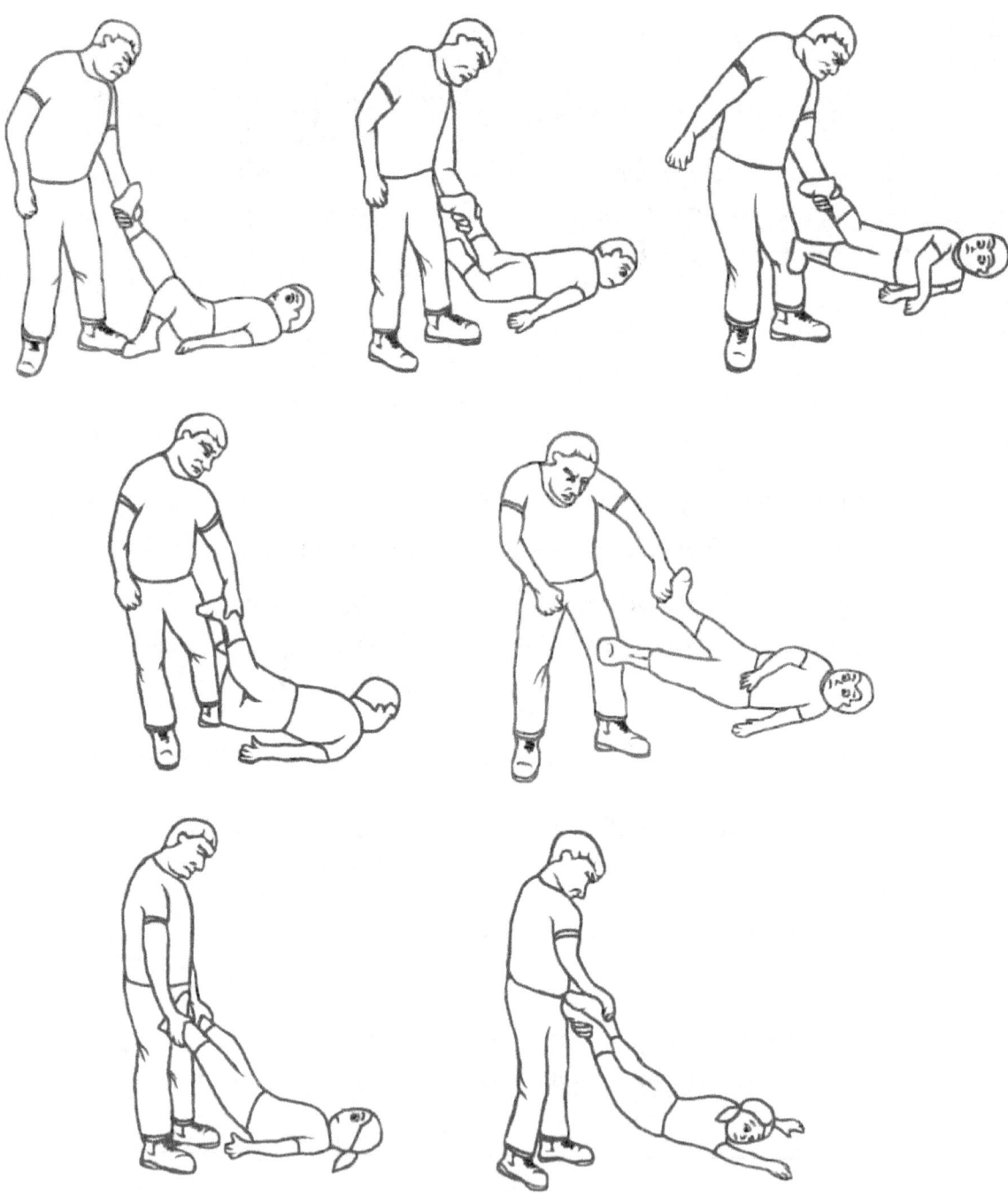

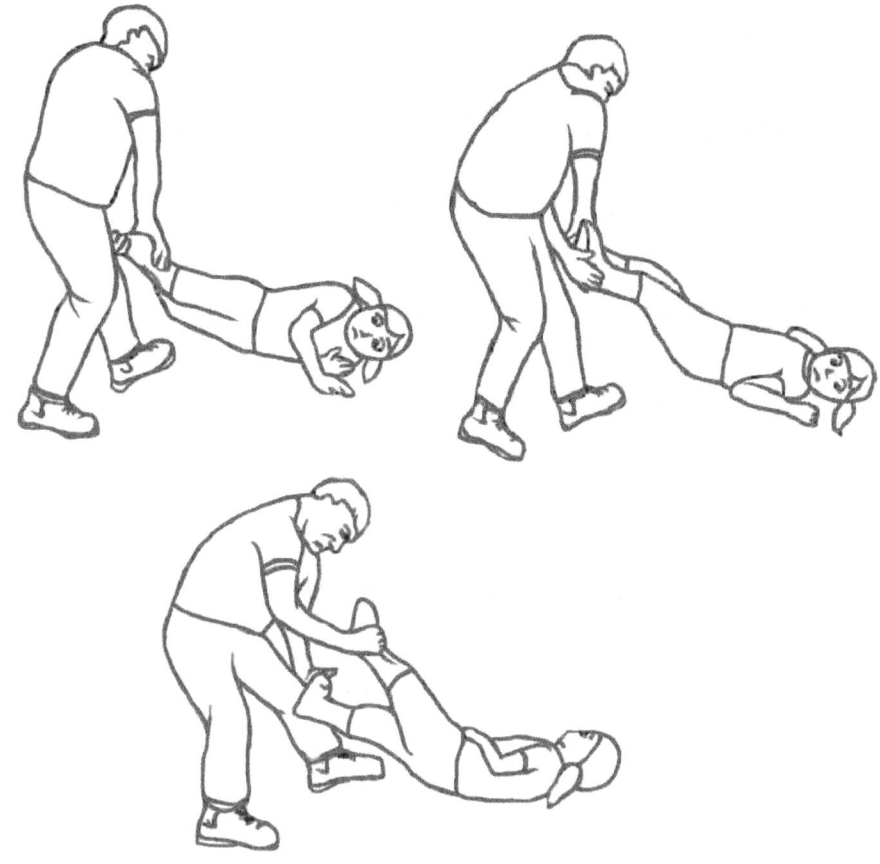

Once their grip on your ankles is released, you can commando crawl, barrel roll or sprint-start run away. If their grip on your ankles is only weakened, you can stamp kick to cause a release and then commando crawl or barrel roll out of arm's reach and sprint-start run away. If one of your legs is free, then you can use it to stamp kick at their fingers or thumb to break their hold on your other ankle and combine this with barrel rolling to break free. Then you can sprint-start run away.

Instructor checklist: make sure your little soldier...

- Barrel rolls multiple times to break the grip on their ankles. They may have to roll several times to one side then change their direction to the other side to break the bad big person's grip.

- If they break one leg free, stamp kicks with their free boot at the bad big person's legs, fingers or thumbs to make them let go.

- When the bad big person's grip is broken, your little soldier can commando crawl, barrel roll or sprint-start run away to safety.

HOW TO PROTECT YOURSELF AGAINST STRIKES

If a bad big person ever tries to hit you with their open hands or fists, then squat-crouch and cover guard, pivot and sprint-run away.

Remember that a "cover guard" is when you raise your forearms and elbows and place the palms of your hands on the back of your neck with your palms around your spinal cord from where it enters your skull and brain downwards. You are trying to protect that part of your neck where your neck and head meet, and as far below that as your hands can cover, as well as from your head and face down to your waist.

With your cover guard firmly in position your forearms and your elbows can protect against incoming strikes or slaps. Squat-crouch so that your elbows are down to your waist so your arms protect you from your head to your waist to cover against incoming strikes or slaps. Squat-crouching helps to make you a hard target.

As soon as it is safe to do so pivot both your boots in the direction of escape and execute your sprint-start evasion and escape. As part of a sprint-start run escape you can pivot your boots to change your position so as to best cover and deflect strikes and slaps. You can also pivot and stamp kick immediately before sprint-run escaping.

If the big bad person tries to strike you from your side, squat-crouch and pivot both boots away from the bad big person while bringing your hands and arms up to form a cover guard as above. Squat-crouch, pivot and sprint-run escape or leg stamp and sprint-run escape as for a front-on attack.

If the bad big person is behind you and hits you and you cannot immediately get away, then step forward and away from the bad big person. Squat-crouch, put your cover guard up, pivot in the direction of your escape and sprint-run away.

Instructor checklist: make sure your little soldier…

- Squat crouches and cover guards by raising the elbows and placing the palms of their hands over the back of their neck. They are trying to protect their spine where their neck meets their head.

- Holds their cover guard firmly in position and uses it to protect against strikes and slaps.

- Squat-crouches so their elbows are down to their waist.

- If the bad big person is in front or behind, slides one boot away from the bad big person.

- As soon as it is safe to do so, pivots away from the bad big person in the direction of evasion and escape and makes a sprint-start run escape to safety.

- Can leg stamp immediately before sprint-start run escaping.

NOT ALL DOGS ARE SAFE

I had a friend who knew that I had trained guard dogs and attack dogs. He asked me to help to train his sister's dog that had been aggressive towards her and towards him. Sadly, before I could contact her, she was killed by her own dog.

Although the chances of being attacked by dangerous dogs are low, if it does happen it is terrible. In the unlikely event that your little soldier is faced by such life-threatening danger, they need to be aware of why and how dogs attack and how they can best avoid, prevent or reduce the risk and extent of injuries if under attack.

Family army instructors, you must understand that dog attacks on anyone are extremely dangerous and can be deadly. That danger is raised to a very high level when children are the victims.

The skills that I teach to adult combatants to neutralise dangerous dogs require high levels of mental toughness, robust physical attributes, improvised weapons and hands-on training. Children simply do not have the physical capabilities to employ skills that would be the best means for a committed realist adult to neutralise a dog attack.

The best means for your little soldiers to prevent a dog attack are to identify dangerous dogs from a safe distance and employ avoidance tactics. This requires that your little soldiers be vigilant, aware of the danger that dogs can be to them and be proactive in avoiding such dogs.

Any roaming dog should be avoided if possible. Avoidance can be as simple as changing direction from a safe distance. If the dog shows aggression and your little soldier cannot safely get completely away, then they should climb up a tree, get behind or on top of a fence, or get up high onto anything that is safe to climb on top of. This way they can stay out of harm's way until help arrives. For a child or young person, these are the preferred methods of threat neutralisation.

For example, if your little soldier can get inside a fenced area and close a gate that the dog can't get through or over it will act as a safety barrier until help arrives.

Getting out of harm's way must be tactically achieved, slowly and carefully. Otherwise, your little soldier's movement may be perceived as prey escaping or as a challenging action, and this may trigger the dog to immediately chase and attack.

I have provided a range of tactics and skills: to avoid dogs that are considered a high risk; to prevent dog attacks; and, if attacked by a dog and no other option is available, counter means and methods to reduce risk as much as possible until help arrives.

So, educate your little soldiers on the dangers of free roaming dogs. Tell them to identify them from as far away as possible and to slowly avoid them by changing direction and taking another route. Tell them that they can return home or go somewhere safe and get help or wait for help.

If they are near a roaming dog that may be protecting its territory and your little soldier cannot tactically avoid the dog, then they must stand completely still. They should stand in a diagonally side-on front stance with their arms locked tight against their sides and with their fists clenched in front of their groin against their inner thighs. Tell them not to eyeball the dog, as the dog may see this as a challenge or threat and tell them to use only peripheral vision to maintain awareness of the dog and its actions.

With any luck, the dog will simply lose interest in your little soldier, and when it is safe the child can slowly back off until they are out of danger.

I have included a range of skills to interfere with a dog's focus, like throwing an object as the dog aggressively approaches or comes into attack. Once the object has been thrown, however, and if it fails to distract the dog, time and distance are against the victim being able to employ another defensive option. As such, I recommend that when an aggressive dog is targeting your little soldier, the primary dangerous dog countermeasure should be to maintain a layer of protection between your little soldier and the attacking dog. This requires immediate decision making by your little soldier to make ready clothing or a backpack to use as a layer of protection against the biting dog.

It is very important that you read through and explain clearly and carefully to your little soldiers the following information in regard to prevention by avoidance. As a last resort emergency-only option against an attacking dog, I recommend counter options by means of offering the dog something else to bite on.

By careful, controlled, tactical placement of the garment or backpack, timed with the dog's incoming bite, the immediate risk can be averted and with luck someone will come to your little soldier's aid. The correct way to do this is detailed in the little soldiers' instructions to follow.

If your little soldier has time and is not in immediate danger, taking their backpack from their back and putting it on the front of their body is a simple transition. If, however, they are in immediate threat of being attacked by a dog the transition must be done as slowly and as discreetly as possible.

Sudden actions or the dropping of the backpack will increase risk and danger.

Instruction on front body positioning of the backpack will be detailed in the upcoming instructions.

Offering the attacking dog something to bite on provides both a layer of protection and secondary options before or after it has latched on. These secondary options include letting the protective layer go as the dog bites it or going with the dog's biting-pulling action and putting up no resistance while maintaining firm footing in a crouched increased-stability stance, or, if the dog is too strong, releasing the grip on the backpack or garment and letting the dog have it.

The most dire and dangerous situation is where the little soldier is under attack but has nothing to offer the dog to bite. This is a life-threatening situation for a child and requires extreme bravery in the face of extreme danger. The best chance of surviving this dangerous dog attack scenario is for the little soldier to become a human rock on the ground, thereby reducing access to their face, throat, nape of the neck, and arms and legs, in the hope that a capable adult comes to their aid or the dog loses interest.

The ground-protection rock-like position above will be detailed later in this section.

After giving your little soldier instructions on how to get ready to deal with an aggressive dog, you can simulate the dog biting by getting down on all fours and then lunging in. Use the web of your hand between your thumb and index finger with your other fingers compressed tightly together to simulate a dog's jaws. By closing your fingers and thumb together you can safely simulate a biting action and your little soldier can employ the preventative and counter canine threat tactics and skills in this manual.

You can make a dog hand puppet to simulate a biting dog. The following are my dog training dog simulators. You can buy something similar or make something to simulate a biting dog.

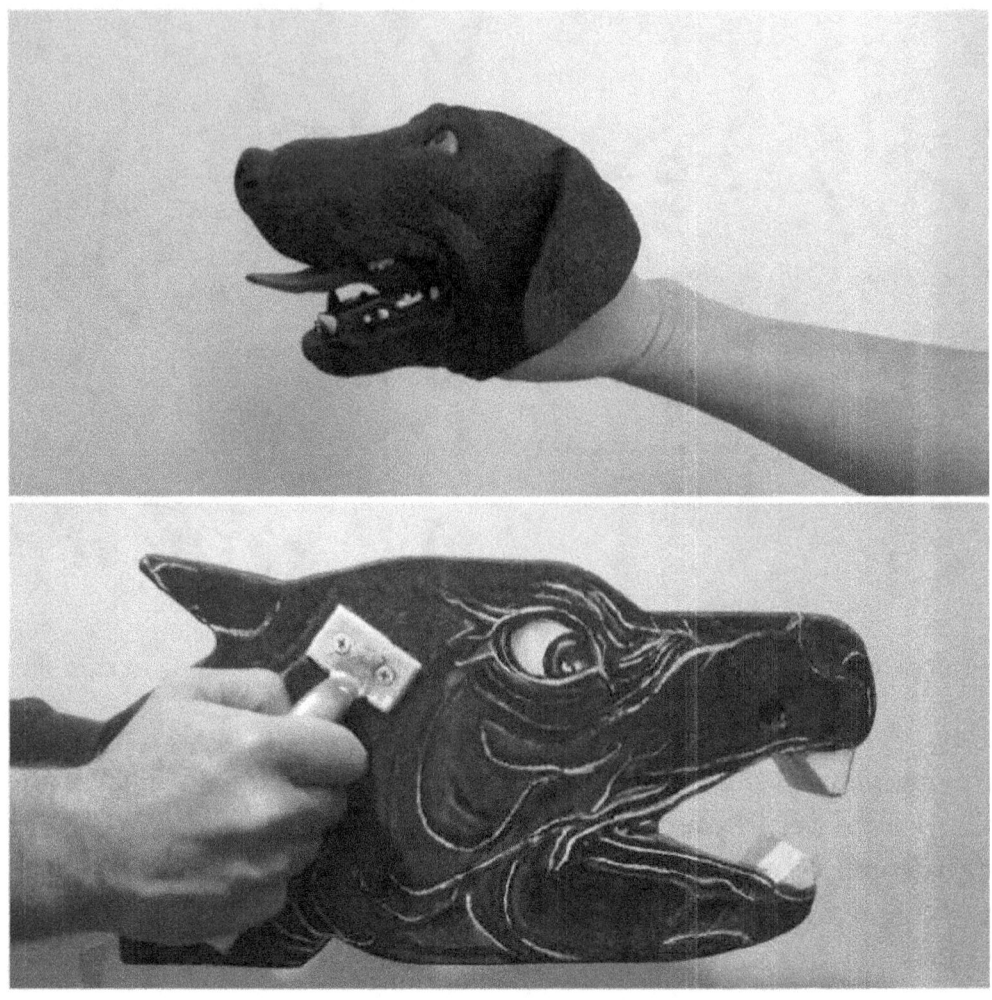

I reiterate, read both the previous and additional family army instructor content and your little soldiers' instructions content and make sure that you understand them and can instruct them clearly and practice the skills so that your little soldiers know exactly what to do.

Slowly and carefully execute the actions of a dangerous dog stage by stage and instruct counter actions part by part.

Let your little soldier know that screaming, running or resisting an attacking dog will only trigger the dog to be more goal-driven and more dangerous. I understand how hard it is for a child not to scream and try to get away when being bitten by an aggressive dog, but the reality is that under such a dire threat their best means of last resort risk reduction survival is to reduce risk by getting into the human rock position detailed later in this chapter and focusing on staying still, staying quiet and using controlled breathing.

I had to think long and hard in regard to providing family army instructors with methods to neutralise a dog that is attacking their little soldier in the case where they come to their little soldier's aid.

There are many methods to dispatch an attacking dog, but most require weapons implementation and training which would most likely not be applicable to an unexpected dog attack on your little soldier. To incapacitate or dispatch a dangerous dog attacking your little soldier requires trained tactics and skills, prior practice and a high level of intestinal fortitude. So, I decided not to include detailed terminal skills in this manual for children's safety. I am sure, however, that a practical realist, given a life-threatening attack on their little soldier and given available weapons or improvised weapons, could dispatch the dangerous dog by deadly means, by destroying its life support capabilities by deliberate penetration or hard impact.

You must understand, however, that if you incapacitate a dangerous dog or force it to release its bite of your little soldier, it will most likely attack you. So, you need to be prepared for that by reading the following carefully.

FAMILY ARMY INSTRUCTOR: METHODS OF BREAKING THE BITE

The following are less-than-lethal options to interfere with either canine life support systems or canine delicate senses, so as to cause a bite release in a dog that has hold of your little soldier.

You need to understand that if you manage to force a release of the bite hold on your child, the dog may simply change its target and start attacking you. So, you may need to include in your dog-bite-release plan a method of muzzling the dog or containing the dog by tying it to something it cannot get away from.

You will have a higher level of safety if you do not have to seize and secure the attacking dog. For example, one option is to spray the dog's eyes and airway with a fire extinguisher or an aerosol spray that interferes with respiration and painfully affects the dog's eyes.

There are nonlethal means of making a dog release the bite on your little soldier, but they require point-blank range bodily contact with the dog. The first method is to choke and strangle the dog until you can make the dog release its bite hold of your little soldier. I will describe how to do this with a lever through the dog's collar first, and then without a lever.

To choke and strangle the dog using a lever through the dog's collar, first straddle the dog from behind. Lock the dog's loin behind the rib cage and forward of the pelvic bone between your legs, insert a lever like a screwdriver or a tyre iron through the dog's collar and use the lever to twist the collar until the dog lets go of the bite or loses consciousness.

Some warnings are in order. First, be aware that if the dog loses and then regains consciousness, it may attack the child again and it may attack you. Second, when seizing and securing a dog from behind, remain vigilant in relation to the dog's head movements and actions. Third, note that when straddling the dog, you may need to adjust your position or hold to maintain safety. Fourth, be aware that if you continue to hold the choke/strangle after the dog has been rendered unconscious, then after a prolonged period of several minutes the dog will most likely die. Fifth, if immediately after the dog releases its bite on the child you maintain the choke and drag the dog and tether it to something, this reduces the risk of a continued dog attack.

To choke and strangle the dog without using a lever through the dog's collar, straddle and secure the dog between your legs as previously and seize the collar with both hands in overhand grips. Pull up and back on the collar and then twist the collar in opposite directions with both hands to achieve the same choking strangling effect and bite release. This method requires more physical strength than does using a lever.

If the dog does not have a collar on, then you can use your belt or any sturdy ligature by putting it under the dog's muzzle and around its neck and tying it securely then employing the same choking means of bite release as previously instructed.

After incapacitating the dog by choking/strangulation, if you have a sturdy bag/sack that you can secure over the dog's head and secure/tie around its neck or to its collar, you can control and contain the dog on the ground, thereby reducing the likelihood of being bitten; a large flexible shopping bag could be used for this. Additionally, tying the dog's front legs together makes containing it safer and more effective; one of your bootlaces could be used for this. When putting a bag over the dog's head, tying its legs or tethering the dog, be sure that the dog cannot get free.

Another means of causing bite release is to use an implement similar to the pictured breaking stick (below) used for separating fighting dogs.

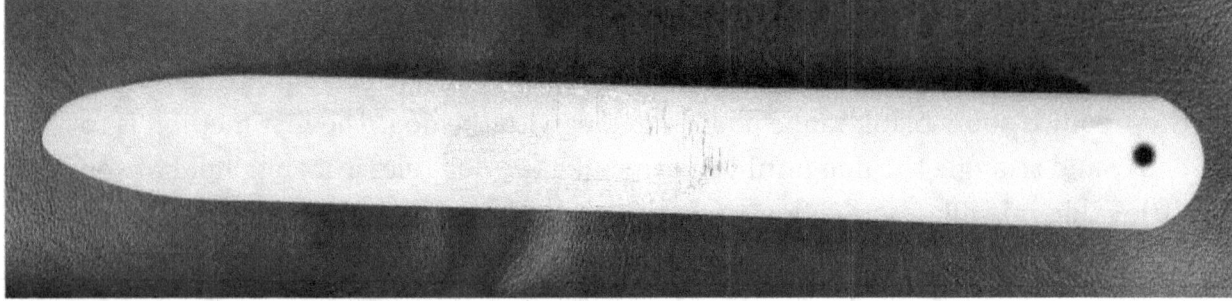

Breaking sticks do not have sharp edges and are somewhat flat shafted. They can be inserted flat and then twisted 90 degrees to side on and used to lever the lower jaw open. A similar effect can be achieved with a screwdriver by once again getting behind the dog and seizing the collar or scruff of the neck. Then, push the screwdriver in behind the canine teeth as far back as possible through any gaps in the pre-molars/molars. Push through between the lower and upper jaws and across towards the opposite side of and up into the upper jaw/roof of the mouth above the gum line. Then twist and lever downwards to force the jaws apart.

The major difference between a purpose-made breaking stick and a screwdriver is that the end of the screwdriver will penetrate the gums of the upper jaw or the roof of the mouth and cause pain as well as leverage, separating the jaws and achieving a release of your little soldier.

The pain of the penetration of the screwdriver tip may cause an immediate bite release but it may also anger the dog so that it turns the attack on you. To reduce this risk, I strongly recommend tethering the dog to something it can't get away from before using an implement to break the bite. You may need to tell your little soldier to move with you as you pull the dog, so that you can tether the dog before using your implement to cause a release of the bite.

You may have to use more than one of the above options to effectively release the dog's bite on your little soldier and to control restrain/contain the dog.

If you can get help from others to assist with tethering or tying the dog's front legs or securing a hood over the dog's head, this will make things easier and safer. Always think, decide and take the time needed to get it right. Do not rush and panic.

Little soldiers, be careful of dogs that you know to be aggressive or biters. Be careful also of dogs that you do not know; you must assume that all unknown dogs are unsafe and could bite you.

Always ask someone if it is safe and alright to pat their dog. If they say yes, then do not extend your arm at first. Instead, let the dog sniff you, and do not make any fast or sudden movements. Once the dog has sniffed and maybe licked your hand, pat it only under the chin, on the front of its neck or on its chest, in a gentle downward palm of hand action. Do not pat it on the head from above or from behind, because in dog thinking, this is a threat, and the dog can get instantly angry if you do this. Be sure to pat it only slowly and gently on its chin, throat or chest.

If you see a roaming dog, remember that it could be guarding its territory and it may see you as a threat. You should avoid it by changing direction or crossing the street slowly, well before you get close to it.

If you cannot change direction or get away before you come in contact with an aggressive dog, then get behind a fence that the dog can't get through or over, or climb a tree or get onto anything where the dog can't get to you. Remember, you can climb, but a dog cannot, and you can open a gate latch, but a dog cannot. So, you are playing to your advantage by doing these things. It can be as simple as opening a gate to a property that is well fenced and safe and staying behind it until you can get help or until someone comes along to help you.

Remember dogs may not be best at climbing but they can jump, so if you climb up a tree or on top of something you need to be above the dogs jumping range.

Dogs can jump and scramble up and over even high fences if the surface provides a positive grip.

So, getting up to a height above 2 metres would be best. You could use branches to provide cover protection against a jumping dog once you get up a tree.

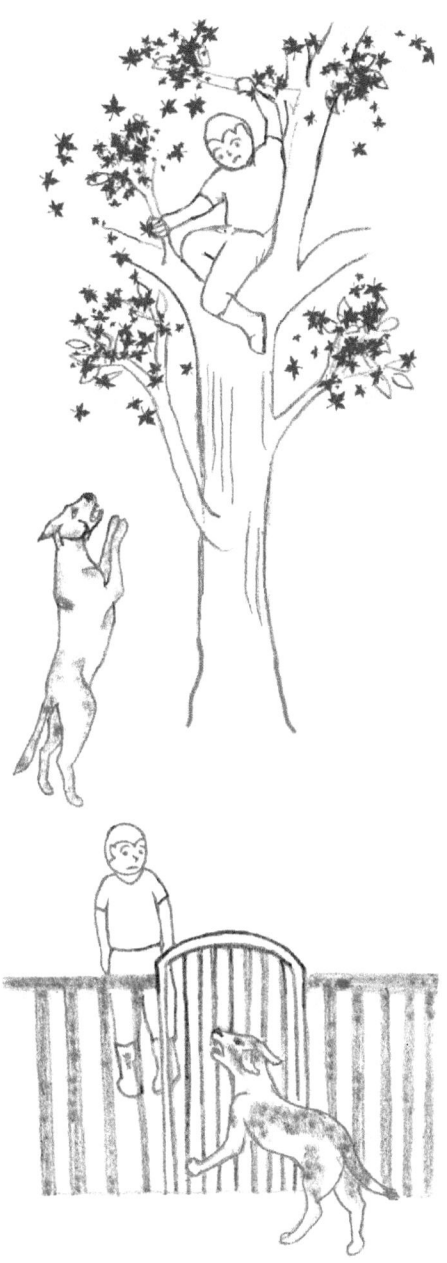

If a dog comes close to you and is growling, barking or showing any aggression towards you, it is important that you stand completely still and turn on your controlled breathing. Inhale through your nose and exhale out of your mouth in a slow intensity controlled breathing cycle. Then decide on the best direction to covertly and very slowly pivot towards, to get into a position to prevent an attack or if attacked to reduce the risk.

This pivot movement will move the front of your body away from the dog placing the outside of your closest thigh to the dog, in line with the dog.

Any time when you are covertly setting a diagonally side on front stance position it must be inch by inch slow motion movement.

Should the dog detect your movement and show increased aggression, you must stop your movement and stand completely still.

Do not look directly at the dog but keep the dog in your vision through peripheral vision, out of the corner of your eye.

If the dog is directly in front of you, you can pivot to either your right or left side to a side-on diagonal front stance.

Make sure you can see the dog out the corner of your eye, and never turn your back on the dog and lose vision of it.

Keep your chin down and inside your shoulder and your arms tight to your sides with your fists clenched down and inside your thighs in front of your groin.

If the dog is in front of you to your left shoulder side pivot both your boots to your right side until you are in a diagonal side-on front stance to the dog as previous where the dog was to your front center.

If the dog is in front of you to your right shoulder side pivot both your boots to your left side until you are in a diagonal side-on front stance with the dog in your peripheral vision.

If you detect a dog behind you from over your right shoulder pivot both your boots to your right to a diagonal side-on-to-the-dog front stance.

If you detect a dog behind you from over your left shoulder pivot both your boots to your left to a diagonal side-on-to-the-dog front stance.

You can make any minor slow motion adjustment movements to increase stability or alignment to the dog by pivoting or sliding footwork.

It is important that you keep the outside muscle side of your closest thigh to the dog in line with the dog.

You must make yourself as streamlined as possible and your delicate bodily vitals and life support systems as protected and away from the dog as possible.

The diagonal side on front stance alignment to the dog is to ensure your outside large muscle groups are closest to the dog and your major arteries, face, throat, back of your neck, spine, abdomen, groin and inner thighs are turned away from the dog and protected by the side large muscle groups of your leg, buttocks and outer upper arm.

NEVER
- Eyeball the dog, or
- Extend your arms or legs out towards the dog, or
- Scream, squeal or yell, or
- Make any sudden, dynamic movements

Maintain your statue like diagonally side on streamlined front stance, continue to use slow, low intensity controlled breathing and maintain discreet vision of the dog out of the corner of your eye (peripheral vision).

If the dog moves, you can covertly pivot your boots to realign to the dog and if need be you can slide your furthermost boot from the dog to reset a stable protected stance. Slow motion inch-by-inch adjustments are a must, with no sudden dynamic large movements.

When the dog is to your front or side after getting into a side-on diagonal front stance, if required to protect your leg furthermost from the dog, slide the boot of that leg slowly and covertly directly back behind your forward leg closest to the dog.

When the dog is behind you after getting into a side-on diagonal front stance, if required for added protection of your leg furthermost from the dog, slide the boot of that leg slowly and covertly directly forward behind your front leg closest to the dog.

If you can move so as to put a barrier between you and the dog, like a fence or a car, then do so. If you have a bike with you, and you can keep your bike sideways in front of you, then this can offer a layer of protection by getting you out of the dog's bite reach.

You could also point your bike front on to the dog, lift the front wheel of the bike off of the ground and turn the handlebars so the front wheel is side on and acts as a barrier to keep the dog away from you. Always stay on the opposite side of the bike frame to the dog.

If you use your bike as a barrier, hold it across in front of you. If the dog attacks you, push the centre of the bike's frame into its biting mouth. Hold the frame or handlebar on the closest side of the bike to you so that the dog has to bite the other side of the bike and cannot bite your hands.

When it bites the steel frame of the bike, it will most likely let go and try to bite again. You will need to continue to use your bike frame as a layer of protection between you and the dog. Think of it like being a knight in armour using his shield.

If you are holding your bike front with the front wheel off of the ground, you can turn the handlebars to position the front wheel in front of the biting dog's muzzle.

If all you have is something small like a handkerchief or baseball cap, then scrunch it up tight in your master hand (that is, the hand that you write with). Then, position your throwing master hand at your side. If the dog goes to bite you, take your fist with the object you will throw in it and throw whatever you have in your hand in front of the incoming dog with a small underhand throwing action. Immediately afterwards, replace your clenched fist against your inner thigh in front of your groin, so as to not leave your hand sticking out to be bitten.

The aim is to take the dog's focus off of biting you and instead redirect its attention onto the closest thing to it, which is the item you have thrown.

Once the dog figures out that whatever you have thrown at it is not something that will fight back, the dog may lose interest in it and focus on you again. You need to keep still and not run away, as the dog will most likely chase and bite you if you move suddenly or run.

As soon as you see a dog, you should be planning and getting ready to protect yourself against being bitten. So, it is important that you get something ready to offer the dog to bite if it attacks, instead of leaving it nothing to bite but you.

Like a big soldier putting on body armour, you need to get your backpack, shirt, jersey, jacket or any item of clothing ready in case the dog attacks.

LAYER OF PROTECTION

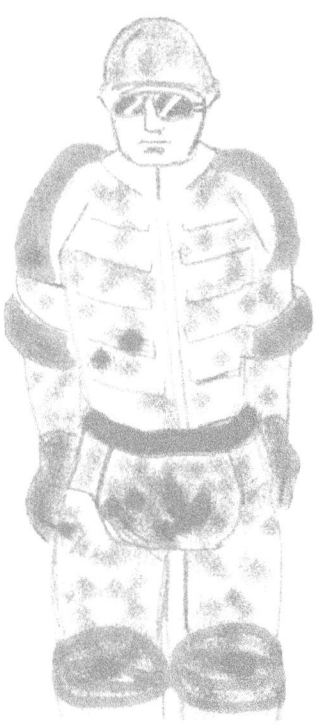

Family army instructor, you now need to take the role of the attacking dog. Get down on all fours and move into range three or four metres away from your little soldier. Instruct them to pivot both boots diagonally forward to keep you, the dog, diagonally to their front and outside and slide their boot on the side they pivoted to diagonally backwards to a diagonal side-on front stance. Make sure they have the outside of their forward leg facing you to protect their groin and the front of their body.

Check they are in the diagonally forward-facing streamlined side-on front stance (arms tight to their sides, fists clenched in against their inner thighs in front of their groin, chin down on their chest). Check that they are using their peripheral vision to remain focused on you, the dog.

Now get them to transition their backpack from their back to their front as per the upcoming instructions.

When they have the backpack in position, move towards them like an aggressive dog. Growl at them as you do so. Instruct your little soldier that when you initiate a forward biting action (with the web of one hand simulating the biting jaws), they are to slightly crouch to increase stability and to push their backpack out in front of them towards you, the incoming simulated aggressive dog.

Instruct them to adjust their positioning immediately before the lunge and bite to ensure that the backpack is right in front of the dog's muzzle. They want bite contact to be in the centre of their backpack that is extended forward away from their body.

If needed, they can use a small movement adjustment by pivoting and sliding their boots, just enough to achieve centre orientation to the simulated dog.

You need to get your little soldier to practice the transition of their backpack from their back to their front slowly and carefully many times over to ensure that they can do it securely. After the backpack has been transferred from your little soldier's back to their front, the following options will be practiced with a simulated dog attack.

The first two options below must be instructed once the simulated dog bite on the backpack has been made. The decided option will be in regard to each little soldiers' capabilities and decision-making abilities.

> 1) If help is close by, then from a slightly crouched ready position, the little soldier should retain the backpack and move forward, putting up no resistance to the attacking dog's bite hold on their backpack.
>
> 2) If the force level threatens your little soldier's stability, instruct them to release their grip on the backpack and to let the dog take it from them.
>
> 3) If, however, your little soldier considers the dog too dangerous from the outset, instruct them to push-throw the backpack at the incoming dog as it makes its lunge at them, before it can bite the backpack. Push-throwing is pushing and swinging the backpack out at the attacking dog and releasing it.

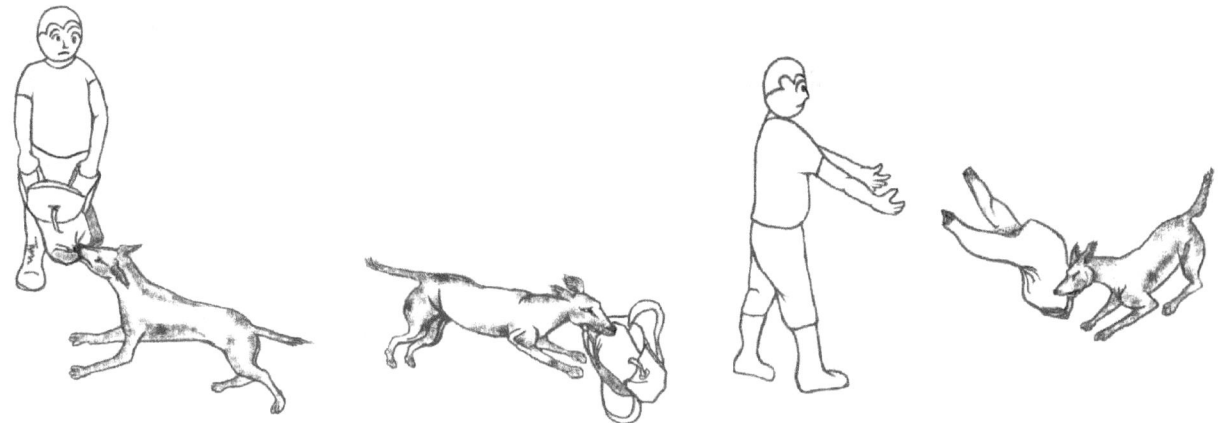

Family Army instructor, now that you have read the outline of using a backpack as a layer of improvised body armour, read the upcoming detailed instructions and practice it yourself before instructing your little soldier. Start with the safe distance simple transferring of the backpack from your little soldier's back to the front of their body, then move on to the slow careful discreet transfer from their back to the front of their body when under close proximity probable canine attack threat.

Little soldiers, you are going to use your backpack as a layer of body armour. If you see a roaming dog some distance from you that could be a danger to you, take your backpack from your back and position it on the front of your body with the shoulder straps over your shoulders and your hands behind the backpack holding the shoulder straps where they are fixed to the bottom of the backpack. This will give you a front protection layer to use to protect yourself should the dog move towards you and attack you. Follow the upcoming instructions and pictures carefully.

Once you have your backpack body armour on the front of your body, should you end up in danger of a dog attack all the hard backpack body armour instructions below apply.

Little soldiers, now you know how to put on and wear your backpack on the front of your body to protect yourself against a dog attack when you have time and distance to safely do so. Now you need to know how to do the same if you are facing an aggressive dog that is close to you. You need to do this covertly (that is, sneakily) moving your backpack from your back to your front. This movement should preferably be made before you get close to a roaming dog. If, however, you are taken by surprise by an approaching dog, then you first set a diagonally side-on front stance to the dog.

If you pivot your boots to the left, then slide your left boot diagonally backwards to a diagonally forward side on right front stance.

If you pivot your boots to the right, then slide your right boot diagonally backwards to a diagonally forward side on left front stance.

Once you are in your diagonally side on front stance then you need to do the following to covertly get your backpack from your back to your front.

<u>If you pivoted to your left</u>, then grasp the top of the right strap of your backpack with your right hand keeping your right arm against your body. Now slide your left hand down and inside the bottom of the left back strap of your backpack against your lower back so that the left back strap slips off of your left shoulder. Using your right hand, slide the right shoulder strap and back of the backpack across the front of your chest and the right shoulder strap over your left shoulder, sliding your left arm inside the right shoulder strap.

Once the backpack shoulder strap is in place over your front left shoulder, use your left hand to grasp the same side bottom shoulder strap behind the backpack against your body. Now release your right-hand grip off the upper shoulder strap and slide your right arm back across behind the back of the backpack and through the right side back strap. Now grasp the bottom of the back strap behind the backpack.

You can adjust the back straps over your shoulders to make sure they are secure by lifting on the bottom back straps behind the backpack and rolling your shoulders forward under the backpack shoulder straps into a secure position over your shoulders.

<u>If you pivoted to your right</u>, grasp the top of the left strap of your backpack with your left hand keeping your left arm against your body. Now slide your right hand and arm down and inside the bottom of the back strap against your lower back so that the right back strap slips off your right shoulder.

Using your left hand, slide the left shoulder strap and back of the backpack across the front of your chest and the left shoulder strap over your right shoulder sliding your right arm inside the left shoulder strap. Once the backpack shoulder strap is in place over your front right shoulder, with your right hand grasp the same side bottom shoulder strap behind the backpack against your body. Now release your left-hand grip of the upper shoulder strap and slide your left arm back across behind the back of the backpack and through the left side back strap. Now grasp the bottom of the back strap behind the backpack.

You can adjust the back straps over your shoulders to make sure they are secure by lifting on the bottom back straps behind the backpack and rolling your shoulders forward under the backpack shoulder straps into a secure position over your shoulders. You can do this on one side or both at the same time, whichever is best for you to do covertly, slowly and securely.

Keep firm downward pressure on the shoulder straps by pulling down on the bottom of the shoulder straps behind the backpack to keep the straps securely in place over your shoulders.

The reason for doing all the slow steady pivoting footwork and handwork when bringing your backpack from your back to your front is to make sure you do not make any sudden moves that might make the dog attack or cause you to drop your backpack. The rule is slow is fast, and never let go with one hand until the other hand has got a secure grip.

Be slow, covert, sneaky and careful as you go, and practice it until you can't make any mistakes. You need to practice making your backpack ready many times before you start to practice with a simulated dog attack on how to use it to protect yourself against an attacking dog.

Practice on your right and left sides until you can transition without getting it wrong. Remember to execute the transition covertly, slowly, carefully, and to always securely keep hold of your backpack straps.

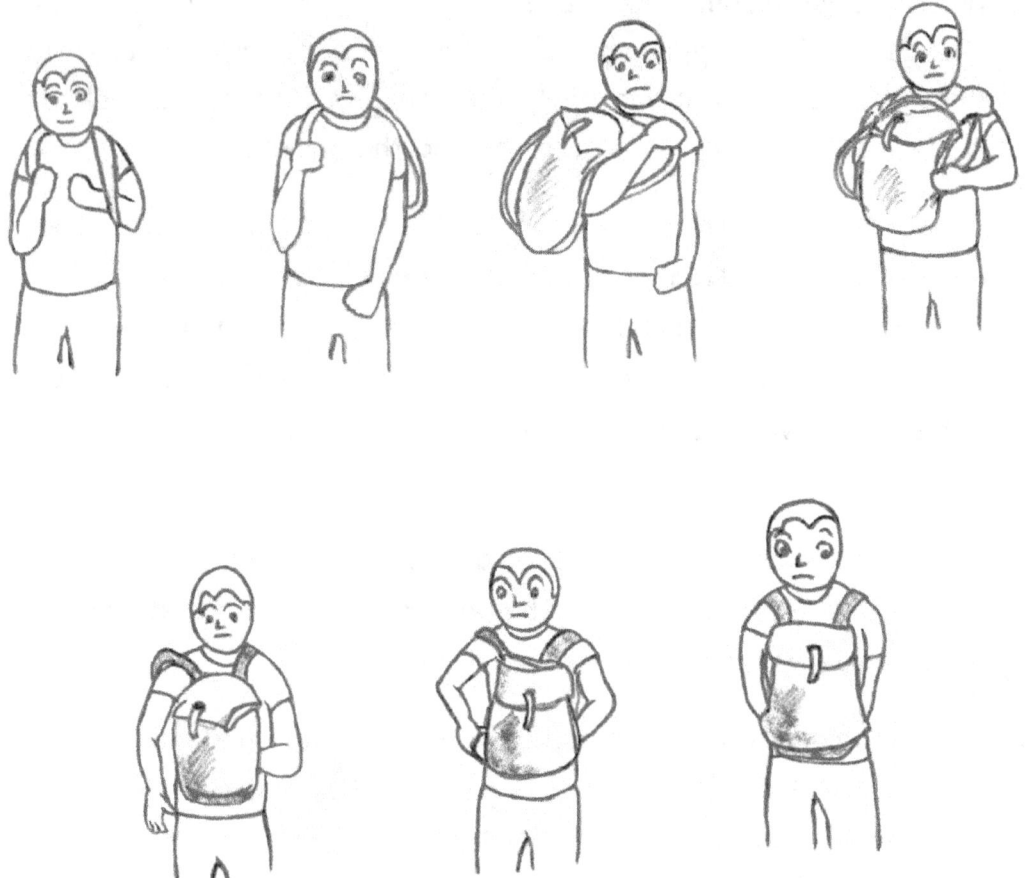

The end result is that your backpack should be positioned flat against your chest and tummy with the straps over your shoulders to your front like you have it on back-to-front.

Grab the shoulder straps close to where they join to the back of the backpack at the bottom and keep your hands behind the backpack holding the straps against your body.

If the dog attacks, loosen your hold on the straps at the bottom of the backpack and slide your hands up the back of the backpack against your body. Grab the shoulder straps of the backpack, slip them forward and off your shoulders, pivot slightly towards the dog if need be and push the backpack at the incoming attacking dog.

When the dog is very close to you and making its lunge and biting movement action, you will use a pushing, swinging and release action away from your body. Push-swing the bottom of the backpack outward and release the backpack right in front of the dog's muzzle.

If the dog is too close or is coming in too fast to enable you to swing and release the bottom of the backpack at the incoming dog, then you can offer the dog the backpack to bite instead of you. To do this, you keep hold of the lower back straps behind the backpack then pivot to line yourself up to the dog if you need to, and then push the bottom centre of the backpack away from your body towards the dog, so that the dog will bite the bottom centre of the backpack and not you. As soon as it bites the backpack, let it go and pivot back to side on and stand still.

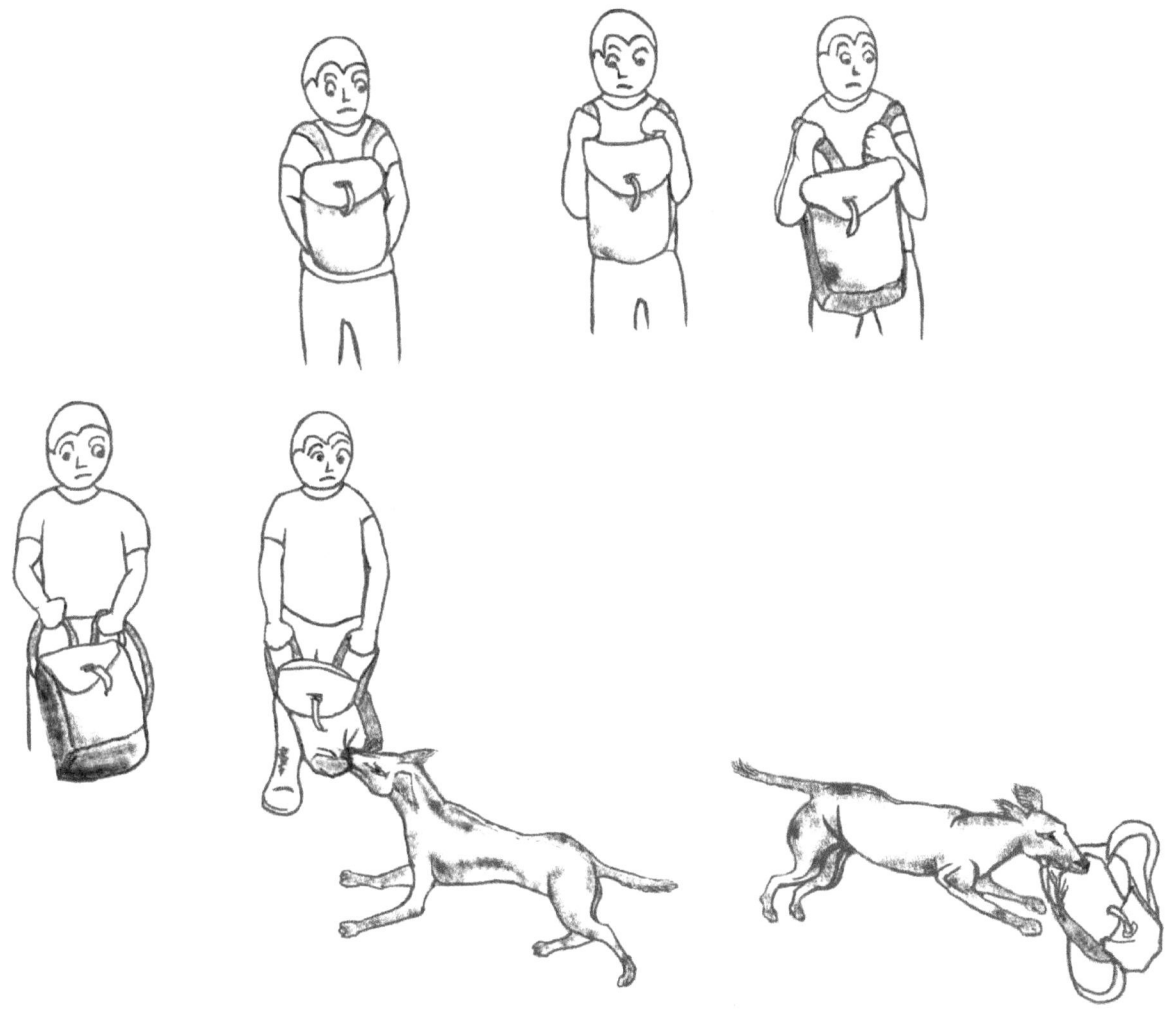

Alternatively, if there are big people nearby who are coming to your aid, you can keep holding onto the backpack, and walk towards the dog after it has locked onto your backpack, yielding to its pulling. Do not resist or pull back, just move with the dog's movement. If you feel you are going to fall over or are in danger of getting bitten, only then release your hold of your backpack and let the dog have it.

You need to practice all the above options many times over until you know you can make the decision and use the best option to keep you as safe as possible.

If you identify a dog some distance in front of you that is not an immediate danger you should transfer your backpack to your front in case the dog comes towards you.

Family army instructor, now that you have instructed your little soldier on how to use their backpack as body armour, you will need to practice using a clothing item instead as a final layer of protection against a biting dog attack.

As per your little soldiers' instructions below, on how to make ready an item of clothing, instruct your little soldier step by step and slowly until they cannot get it wrong.

This means high-repetition practice of setting a slightly crouched diagonally forward side-on front stance, keeping the dog to their front and making the clothing item covertly ready as a layer of protection between your little soldier and the simulated dog attack. Be sure they learn how to pivot and slide their footing to adjust to the dog's position.

You will again need to get down on all fours, several metres away from your little soldier and simulate aggressive dog behaviour. Instruct your little soldier as before to set a side-on diagonally forward-facing streamlined slightly crouched front stance and to carefully and covertly make ready an item of clothing as per their provided instructions.

Once they have the item of clothing firmly in position, move towards them, simulating an aggressive dog, and then lunge and use the web of one hand to simulate the bite.

As you simulate the first bite, have them swing the centre of the clothing towards the simulated bite. This will most likely require them to pivot towards the incoming dog attack simulation in a crouched stance to increase stability.

To increase stability or for movement, have them slide their boots to change the width or depth of their stance.

Now, as previously, have your little soldier practice their post-bite backpack options, but with the item of clothing. They can immediately push-throw the item of clothing as the dog makes its biting lunge, or, as soon as the bite is secured on the clothing, let the clothing go. Alternatively, they can move forward with the simulated biting and tugging, offering no resistance and letting go of the clothing only when they fear being bitten or if their stability is at risk.

Practice high repetitions from different angles of approach so that your little soldier learns how to transition from diagonally side on to facing and being centred to the simulated dog lunge and biting action.

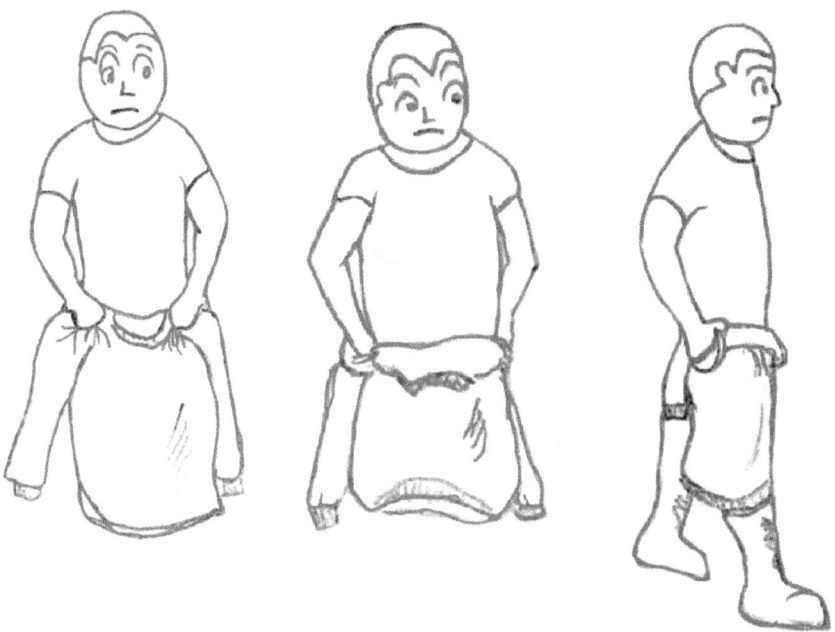

Little soldiers, if you do not have a backpack but you do have a shirt, jersey, jacket or any other item of clothing, this is how to make it ready to provide you with a layer of protection against an attacking dog.

You don't want to make any sudden big movements, so make your item of clothing ready by standing still and turning diagonally side on to the dog, just as you did with your backpack. With a shirt, jersey or jacket, grasp it close to top of both sleeves and covertly, as slowly and carefully as you can, stretch the clothing around in front of your body until both your hands and forearms are at your sides.

Now as slowly and as covertly as possible, which remember means as sneakily as you can, wrap the sleeve once around your hand and securely re-position your hand against your side. Now wrap the other sleeve once around your other hand and securely re-position that hand against that side.

Pull the clothing like a rope firmly around in front of your body. You want your hands holding the clothing at your sides with your arms bent and tight against your sides, elbows back and the clothing positioned tight across the front of your body. Your hold on the clothing needs to be secure but it also needs to enable you to be able to release your grip and let the clothing unwind from your hands if need be.

You will need to practice this set-up position until you can't get it wrong. Make sure you know where to grasp the sleeve so that after you have wrapped it once around your securely holding fists it is positioned firmly against your body.

If the dog attacks, push the clothing at the dog as it lunges to bite by slightly crouching and pivoting slightly to centre yourself to the dog if you need to and offering the centre of the outstretched clothing for the dog to bite. You need to be very brave and hold the middle of the clothing out towards the centre of the dog's jaws as it bites.

The idea is that you want to give the dog something to bite on other than yourself, but you do not want to excite the dog by resisting and making it bite and pull harder. So, you have two options once the dog bites hold of the clothing.

Option 1

By sliding your boots, move slowly and carefully towards the dog as it bites and pulls on the clothing. Putting up no resistance, you can release your grip on the clothing if you feel you cannot stay on your feet and then turn diagonally side on to the dog and stand still again.

Option 2

To protect against being bitten, and if you cannot hold onto the clothing and move towards the dog while the dog tugs at the clothing, you can instead offer the centre of the outstretched clothing and as the dog bites hold of it, you can immediately let the clothing go. After releasing your hold on the clothing, pivot back to diagonally side on and stand still.

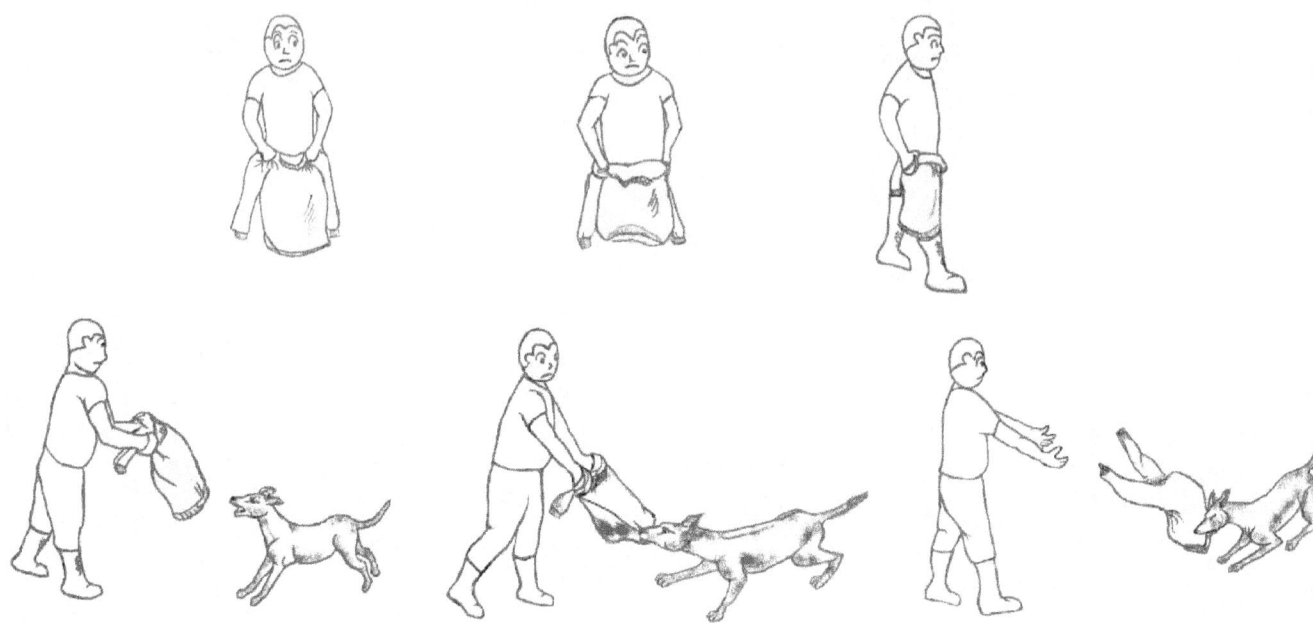

Never turn your back on the dog. Stand in a diagonally side-on front stance to the dog with your chin tucked down on your chest, your head dipped down with your eyes looking away at the ground. Look at the dog out of the corner of your eye. Yes, use your peripheral vision as it is known by big people in your family army, so you have vision of the dog but are not challenging it by staring directly at it.

Stand still and stay silent, always using low-intensity cycled breathing in through your nose and out through your mouth. Stay focused, still and silent until the dog loses interest in you or until someone comes along who can assist you.

Keep your arms tight to your sides with clenched fists inside the top of your thighs covering your groin. Do not squeal or scream like a small animal under attack as this might make the dog attack you.

If you fall over, or if the dog knocks you over, or if the dog is attacking you and you have nothing to offer the dog to bite, then you are in extreme danger. In this case, you must reduce the dangers of bites by protecting as much of your body as possible and leaving nothing outstretched for the dog to bite.

On the ground you need to make yourself like a rock. Kneel down on both knees with your lower legs flat on the ground and your upper legs and buttocks tight on top of your lower legs. Bend forward at the waist and wrap the palms of your hands around the back of your neck. Lower your head and arms down to the ground and tuck your head in with your face inside your arms on the ground. The top hand must be over where your neck enters the back of your skull and the other hand immediately below it with your forearms covering your ears. You must cover all or as much of your upper back, neck, ears and sides of your head as possible. Lock your arms in tight against the sides of your body.

Make sure that nothing is sticking out that the dog can bite. Do not interlace your fingers; doing so leaves 10 tempting sausage-like fingers sticking out to be bitten. Instead, practice right now by putting your palms of your hands behind your neck and covering as much of your neck as you can from the bump where your spinal cord enters your skull down as far as you can cover with both palms of your hands, one above and one below the other (see picture). The dog may try to bite you in various places, and you may need to respond by slowly and covertly adjusting your hand or arm positions to better protect your neck or ears. For example, your inner wrists should cover your ears and not be under them (remember, many dogs have animal ears as chew toys, or have bitten other dogs ears, so your ears are very tempting to them).

Do not be surprised if the dog starts circling around you, poking at you, nipping at you, looking for a way in. Do not be surprised if it tries to jump up on you. It may try to get you for seconds or a minute or two, but it might seem much longer to you, hunched down and under attack. So, be patient; if you act like a rock, you will be as boring as a rock!

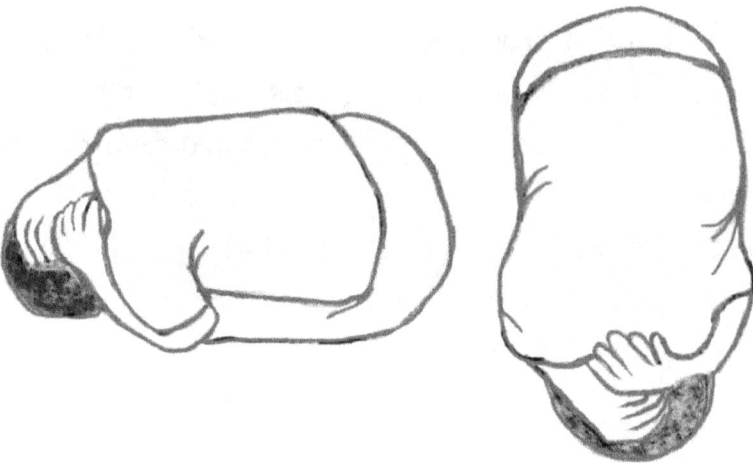

Be brave and breathe in through your nose and out through your mouth slowly and keep as still as you can, no matter how afraid you are or even if you feel a lot of pain. Silently say to yourself "I must be a brave little soldier, yes rock solid!"

Try your hardest not to move or scream, because the best way to stop the dog from biting is to not move, struggle or scream. If the dog gets no fight back, no struggle and no panic movement and there are no screams or sounds like those of a frightened injured animal, it might just get bored, lose interest and walk away.

You need to make sure the dog cannot bite your neck, throat, face, ears, arms or legs. Getting into your hard-cover ground-rock position will reduce bites to these parts of your body and with luck, some big person will come to help you.

If you have your backpack on your back and are on the ground under a dog attack, leave your backpack on your back in your rock position. Then, if the dog bites at your back, your backpack provides a layer of protection.

Remember, your best chance of stopping such an attack is if the dog loses interest in you or if people come to your aid.

FINAL ADVICE FOR LITTLE SOLDIERS

Little soldiers, you are probably asking yourself "what about *this*?" or "what about *that*?" You may even be doubting whether you can get away from a bad big person or an angry dog.

Remember, however, to always use your strengths. For example, you are smaller and nimbler than a bad big person, so make yourself smaller again by squat-crouching and then stamp kicking them low and hard at your level. If sprint-running away from a bad big person, keep your arms close to your body, so that you don't give the bad big person anything to grab hold of. Remember, you can climb a tree higher than a dog can jump. You can open a gate and close it behind you for safety. A dog acts on impulses and instinct, so you need to use your brain to outsmart it. The best option is seeing the dog early and avoiding it if possible.

If, however, you end up on the ground under a dog attack, then make yourself into a rock and know and believe that this is the best option you have to reduce risk and injuries until the dog loses interest or help arrives. These are just some examples of using your strengths.

You need to know the best skill to counter the threat and you need to be able to execute it with confidence and competency. This means that once you have learnt a skill, you must practise it with high repetitions until you simply cannot get it wrong. A high level of skill comes only through training.

INSTRUCTOR TRAINING PROGRAM FOR YOUR LITTLE SOLDIERS

Family army instructors, work through the individual skills from the skills training program in this manual until you have instructed your little soldiers in all of them, and they have achieved confidence and competency.

Once your little soldiers have learned all the tactics and skills, you can randomly select skills from the training program section at the back of this manual and have them practice the selected skill by individual single repetition, or multiple repetitions.

Instruct them to assess threats, decide on how to best and most safely prevent or counter the threat and how to set up and neutralise the threat with the tactics and skills they have learnt.

Get them to know the tactics and skills by name so that they can execute tactics and skills to your command and instruction. For example, "commando side fall and stamp kick," a "standing stamp kick" or a "ground stamp kick," etc.

CONTINUATION TRAINING EXERCISES

The way to increase your little soldiers' confidence is through continued practice. This practice enables your little soldiers to gain in competency and confidence. It also brings familiarity that allows them to develop higher-level physicality and skills-momentum capabilities in training.

Rather than practicing static individual drills for this post-course completion continuation training, I have opted for both static and walking movement practical scenario skills practice.

This practice is important for your little soldiers to be able to develop threat recognition/identification capabilities and as such to decide on best threat neutralisation based on prior training.

This continuation training must be in line with bad big person threat realities so as to best prepare your little soldiers to be able to recognise the threat as early as possible, make the best threat neutralisation decision and effectively execute it to prevent, escape or counter the threat.

The order of execution is based on the safest and best specific threat neutralisation means and methods.

The term "threat neutralisation" equates to all means of threat prevention including anti-threat tactics such as avoidance. It also includes immediate faced threat prevention by evasion and escape or counter action skills.

The counter action skills include resistance combined with counter stamp kicks and escape as well as seizure and abduction prevention and counter action escape.

It is important that family army instructors ensure that specific threats in training are realistic to the actions of bad big person threats on children.

Always ensure that training practices are safe by checking that the training environment is safe and that enemy person physicality is safe and at controlled-force levels. If in doubt in regard to safety during training, then stop, disengage and reset at a safe level and under safe conditions. This includes stopping if the enemy person loses their balance, to ensure they do not fall on their training partner.

Slow and low speed and intensity at a learning level is the correct modus operandi.

Increases in speed and intensity must be at careful and controlled levels.

TRAINING PRACTICE

I reiterate, role-play where you conduct yourself as a bad big person targeting children with practical realism is very important. When approaching your little soldier, use deception, especially in verbiage and reasoning. As an enemy person, all your actions have to be believable and in line with the actions of bad big people who have the intention of abducting children and doing them harm.

It is important that your little soldiers can deal with suspicious deceptive approaches as well as sudden surprise actions. So, as well as using cunning and deception under your enemy person approach and when communicating with your little soldier, you should alternately use sudden shock-action seizure and abduction attempts.

Put on an academy award–winning bad big person role-play performance. This will best familiarise your little soldier with threat awareness, threat recognition and identification which will best enable them to make the safest and best threat neutralisation tactics and skills employment decisions.

Cunning, deception and a pleasant, nice person persona followed by sudden surprise shock actions will increase your little soldiers' threat processing decision-making and threat-neutralisation capabilities through training and practice familiarisation.

If your little soldier is using previously instructed tactics to make themselves a hard target and as such you are having difficulty getting close to them and convincing them that you are a nice person, then changing to a sudden surprise-action seizure and abduction attempt will provide realism to the threat.

Try to get your little soldier to drop their guard by relating to them in a believable way. Suggestions to achieve this include the following: Approach your little soldier and ask for help, telling them that you have lost your reading glasses and that you cannot see the numbers on your mobile phone. If they assist you, then seize them. Use believable everyday verbiage like "can you show me where the supermarket is?" or "I am lost, can you tell me where I am?" or "I've lost my little puppy, she is black and white, have you seen her?" Use your bad big person imagination and be convincing.

Use deception in your movement. For example, make like you are just going to walk right past them and are unaware of their presence, and then suddenly attempt to seize and abduct them. Make sure you practice your approaches and your seizure and abduction attempts from their front, both sides and their rear flanks. Be sure to vary the range from your little soldier that you initiate seizure and abduction attempts.

The following table is a program outline for family army instructors to follow that will give you a varied range of threat types and variations of specific threat types to employ during practical scenario training.

Once you have worked through these training drills with your little soldier from a stationary position, you can introduce walking drills where your little soldier and the enemy person are both on the move. When the bad big enemy person approaches and uses cunning and deception to seize and abduct the little soldier or sudden surprise shock-action in the initiation of seizure of your little soldier, your little soldier will need to quickly assess, decide and execute evasion and escape or threat counter actions.

I have provided a specific threat for initial threat neutralisation scenario training practice statically followed by additional threats from the same threat category.

This provides your little soldiers with the chance to use the same primary means of threat neutralisation against same-category similar threats.

Your little solider should use their prior taught methods of threat prevention tactics or counter threat skills to neutralise the threat.

If they are unsure about any aspect of decision making and tactics and skills execution, you will be able to show them the primary means of threat neutralisation from the little soldiers' primary threat neutralisation required actions. Then you can repeat the threat employment so they can execute the primary means.

Then move on to employ threat category threat variations so that your little soldier can practice their same threat neutralisation skills against similar threats.

I have included an enemy party advice/suggestions component to assist enemy party family army instructors with the set up and employment of threats.

Remember, slow is fast and less is more in training and when learning to enhance the retention of tactics and skills.

Be patient and provide remedial training where required to ensure that your little soldiers have a positive experience and always can make primary decisions and have the opportunity to employ primary threat neutralisation options from their prior training. Make sure skills are executed from the squat crouch position to make your little solider a harder target and always combine the squat-crouch and execution of skills with low-intensity cycled respiration, inhale via the nose with the set-up/squat-crouch and exhale via the mouth with the skill initiation. All continued counter action skills will include self-defence respiration except for sprint running evasion and escape that requires normal running respiration.

Only move on to walking movement drills when you feel your little soldier has achieved competency and confidence and sufficient practise of scenarios in a static/stationary position.

Specific Threat	Primary Threat Neutralisation	Threat Variations, and Enemy Party Suggestions
Suspicious approach front/side/rear.	Evasion and escape.	Silent approach. Asking for directions. Asking to help find a puppy. Wanting to show a phone/toy/tablet.
Suspicious approach to close to body contact range.	Break a 2–3 metre diagonally rearward gap for safety then evasion and escape.	Appearing not to notice little soldier but closing in. Moving slowly then speeding up when close to body contact range with your little soldier. Approaching and asking for help with phone use or reading a sign or instructions.
Suspicious approach combined with surprise action seizure attempt.	Squat-crouch, pivot and evade and escape.	Slow approach fast closing in grab attempt. Closing in yell "stop," or "wait there" and attempt a grab. Yell "watch out, look behind you," or "be careful" combined with a fast approach and grab attempt.
Sudden surprise action single hand clothing or wrist grab.	Squat-crouch, resist, pivot, stamp kick and evade and escape.	Slow approach look away then rapid closing in and grab attempt. Ask little soldier to come here and then attempt to grab them. Crouch like in pain and ask little soldier for help then make a grab at them.

Specific Threat	Primary Threat Neutralisation	Threat Variations, and Enemy Party Suggestions
Suspicious approach combined with surprise action close range single or both hands seizure attempt.	Squat-crouch, resist, pivot and evade and escape.	Say "look at that" and point in a direction away from the little soldier and then make a sudden move and grabbing action. Approach ask for help finding lost reading glasses and then make a grab attack.
2–3 metre unexpected surprise action seizure attempt.	Squat-crouch, pivot, evade and escape.	Look behind yourself then turn back to face little soldier and rush and grab attempt.
Body seizure hold.	body hold from the back, resist, squat-crouch, stamp kick or adjust/pivot stamp kick and evade and escape.	Arms free or secured. One arm free one arm secured. Both shoulders grabbed front or behind.
Body seizure lift and abduction attempt.	Squat-crouch, ground fall resistance, ground stamps kicks, evasion and escape.	Arms free or secured. One arm secured one arm free.
Body seizure abduction ground counter prevention.	Hit-the-deck ground fall, wrap arms and legs around bad big person's legs to prevent abduction, cross ankles, ground leg stamp and evade and escape.	Front, side and rear seizure. Arms free or secured.
Body seizure lift and carry abduction counter belly to belly.	Arms around bad big person to prevent back falling and enable downward pole sliding, one leg wrap around, kneeing groin, thumb-spiking eyes.	Arms free or secured. One arm free, one arm secured. Lift little soldier and hold off ground stationary and or lift and move them.

Specific Threat	Primary Threat Neutralisation	Threat Variations, and Enemy Party Suggestions
High body seizure lift and carry abduction counter from rear.	Hard squat-crouch, upward and downward heel kicks, torso downward, monkey walk or ground fall, commando crawl and backward stamp kicks. Sprint-run escape.	Arms free or secured. Belly to back. One arm free, one arm secured.
Body seizure lift and carry abduction counter from the side, front or rear when the little soldier can hit the deck.	Hard squat-crouch, body drop to stomach, wrap both arms around leg and both legs around bad big person's leg, ground leg stamp, evasion and escape.	Arms free or secured.
Slapping, striking, kicking counter action.	Squat-crouch, hard cover guard, pivot and evasion and escape or pivot, stamp kick and escape action.	Front, side or rear.
Surprise rear grab push or pull.	Squat-crouch, front stance, resist, stamp kick or adjust/pivot stamp kick set up and execution and evade and escape.	Grab hair, shoulders, upper arms, back of neck and upper arm or wrists.

EPILOGUE

The content of this manual has been carefully decided upon and specifically developed to give your little soldiers a primary means of threat prevention and as a last resort under-threat counter actions.

Nothing is guaranteed under threat and the odds are even less when a child is under threat of a bad big person with bad intentions.

The included tactics and skills were carefully and painstakingly developed or are modified versions of military self-defence or military close quarters combat tactics and skills from our military elite training packages.

The skills must be trained until the correct decision in regard to neutralising the faced threat can be made by your little soldier and can be executed with confidence and competency.

This means high-repetition practice and slow careful increases in threat reality and intensity.

In the words of the late military unarmed combat and military self-defence Master-Instructor SGM Harry Baldock, "training is a task to be continued, not a project to be completed."

So, when you have completed all the training from this manual, start over with an emphasis on increased surprise, cunning, deception and different training environments and means and methods of employing threats by thinking like a bad big person intent on abducting and doing harm to a child.

Finally, always instruct, train and practice with safety being paramount. This includes ensuring your little soldiers are well informed and understand all their training responsibilities in relation to safety.

OTHER TITLES BY GEOFF "TANK" TODD

- Brain to Boot: Military CQC & Military Self Defence Psychological Enhancement & Conditioning Manual

- Declare War Against Rape: Military Combative Methods to Neutralise Extreme Sexual Violence

- Military Close Combat Systems Phase One: Offensive and Counter Offensive Unarmed Assault

- No Nonsense Self Defence

- The Do's and Don'ts of Self Defence

- Wheelchair Self Defence with John Marrable

- Tactical Control and Restraint

www.ingramcontent.com/pod-product-compliance
Lightning Source LLC
Chambersburg PA
CBHW080848010526
44114CB00018B/2395